I0466495

Book Description

The Deceiver's Playbook: Inside the World of Scams and Cons

Dive into the shadowy world of scams and cons with *The Deceiver's Playbook*, a gripping exploration of deception that will leave you both shocked and enlightened. From street-level hustles to high-stakes frauds, this book unravels the intricate strategies and psychological manipulations used by scammers to fleece their victims.

In *The Deceiver's Playbook*, you will journey through riveting real-life case studies, revealing the dark genius behind history's most infamous scams. Meet master con artists who charmed their way into high society, only to orchestrate elaborate heists and fraudulent schemes. Discover the vulnerabilities that scammers exploit, and learn how they adapt to modern technology to stay one step ahead of the law.

Each chapter delves into different facets of the con game:

- Love and Deception: Uncover the emotional manipulations in romance scams.
- The Voice of Deception: Learn about phone scams and how they prey on trust and urgency.
- The Dark Web: Explore the hidden corners of the internet where scammers thrive.
- The Hospital Hustle: See how health-related scams target our deepest fears.

But *The Deceiver's Playbook* is more than just a collection of shocking tales. It equips you with the knowledge to protect yourself and your loved ones. With practical tips and insights, you'll learn to recognize red flags, secure your personal information, and stay vigilant against the ever-evolving threat of scams.

This book is a must-read for anyone wanting to understand the dark art of deception and arm themselves against it. Whether you're fascinated by true crime, interested in psychology, or simply want to safeguard your future, *The Deceiver's Playbook* offers a compelling and comprehensive look at the world of scams and cons.

Join the thousands of readers who have been captivated and educated by *The Deceiver's Playbook*. Prepare to be enthralled, enlightened, and empowered.

The Deceiver's Playbook: Inside the World of Scams and Cons

Foreword

In a world where trust is a precious commodity, and deception lurks around every corner, understanding the art of the con has never been more essential. The rise of digital technology and the interconnectedness of our lives have given scammers unprecedented access to potential victims, making their schemes more pervasive and sophisticated. It is within this context that *The Deceiver's Playbook: Inside the World of Scams and Cons* emerges as a vital guide for navigating the treacherous waters of modern-day fraud.

As someone who has dedicated a significant portion of my career to studying criminal behavior and cybersecurity, I have seen firsthand the devastating impact that scams can have on individuals and communities. From the elderly couple who lose their life savings to a slick-talking phone scammer, to the ambitious professional whose career is derailed by a phishing attack, the human cost of deception is immense. This book shines a light on these dark corners, offering both a detailed exploration of scams and practical advice for avoiding them.

The journey through *The Deceiver's Playbook* is both riveting and educational. Each chapter meticulously dissects different types of scams, providing insights into the minds of the con artists who perpetrate them. You will meet master deceivers who exploit emotions, trust, and the allure of easy money. You will learn about the psychological tricks they use to manipulate their victims, and the sophisticated techniques they employ to stay ahead of the law.

One of the most compelling aspects of this book is its focus on real-life case studies. These stories not only illustrate the diverse range of scams out there but also highlight the adaptability and creativity of scammers. From street-level hustles to high-tech frauds, these accounts are a stark reminder of the lengths to which con artists will go to achieve their ends.

But *The Deceiver's Playbook* is more than a collection of cautionary tales. It is a call to action. In these pages, you will find practical strategies for protecting yourself and your loved ones from the myriad threats that exist today. Whether you are a seasoned professional or someone who simply wants to safeguard their personal information, the advice and tips provided here are invaluable.

We live in an age where information is both a tool and a weapon. *The Deceiver's Playbook* equips you with the knowledge needed to defend yourself against the predators of the digital age. It empowers you to recognize red flags, secure your data, and maintain a healthy skepticism in a world where deception is all too common.

As you embark on this journey through the world of scams and cons, I encourage you to absorb the lessons within these pages and share them with others. Together, we can create a more informed and vigilant society, better equipped to thwart the efforts of those who seek to deceive and defraud.

With this foreword, I invite you to delve into *The Deceiver's Playbook*—a compelling, enlightening, and essential read for anyone looking to stay one step ahead in the game of deception.

Dedication

To all the victims of scams and cons, whose stories often go untold. Your resilience and courage inspire this work.

To my family and friends, whose unwavering support and encouragement have been my guiding light.

And to the countless individuals who tirelessly fight against fraud and deception, may this book be a testament to your relentless efforts in making the world a safer place.

This book is for you.

The Deceiver's Playbook: Inside the World of Scams and Cons

Table of Contents

Chapter 1: The Art of Deception

I remember the first time I realized the power of a lie. It was a simple, almost innocent moment in my childhood. I was eight years old, and I had just broken my mother's favorite vase while playing soccer indoors. Fear gripped me as I looked at the shattered pieces scattered across the floor. When my mother asked what happened, I told her that the wind had blown it off the shelf. She believed me. That moment planted a seed in my mind, a seed that would grow into a life of deception and manipulation.

The Beginnings

My name is Marcus Green, and I am a professional scammer. Over the years, I have mastered the art of deception, turning it into a lucrative career. It wasn't always like this. I grew up in a modest household, with parents who worked hard to make ends meet. Despite their efforts, we often struggled financially. It was during these times of struggle that I began to see the world through a different lens.

In high school, I was the kid who could talk his way out of anything. I discovered that people wanted to believe what they were told, especially if it made their lives easier. I honed my skills through small, harmless cons. I sold fake raffle tickets, forged signatures on permission slips, and even managed to convince my classmates that I had an uncle who was a famous movie director. These early cons were my training ground, a place to practice and refine my techniques.

The Turning Point

The turning point came in my early twenties. I was working a dead-end job, barely making enough to pay the rent. I knew I had to do something drastic to change my circumstances. That's when I met Derek, a seasoned con artist who saw potential in me. Derek took me under his wing and introduced me to the world of professional scamming.

Derek taught me the importance of preparation and research. He showed me how to identify potential marks, those individuals who were susceptible to manipulation. We targeted the lonely, the greedy, and the desperate. People who were looking for a quick fix to their problems. We promised them what they wanted to hear, and they believed us because they needed to believe us.

The First Big Score

My first big score was a classic Ponzi scheme. Derek and I set up a fake investment firm, complete with a professional-looking office and a slick website. We promised high returns on investments, guaranteeing that their money would double within six months. We even had a few "clients" – friends of Derek – who vouched for our success.

The money started pouring in. People invested their life savings, trusting us with their future. We used the initial investments to pay off earlier investors, creating an illusion of legitimacy. As word spread, more and more people wanted to invest. It was exhilarating and terrifying at the same time. The thrill of the con was intoxicating, but the fear of being caught was always lurking in the background.

After six months, with millions in our accounts, Derek and I vanished. We closed the office, shut down the website, and disappeared without a trace. The fallout was brutal. People lost everything, and the authorities launched a massive investigation. But we were long gone, living comfortably in a tropical paradise.

The Evolution of the Scam

Over the years, I evolved. The scams became more sophisticated, the stakes higher. I delved into identity theft, credit card fraud, and even corporate espionage. Each con required meticulous planning and execution. I surrounded myself with a network of skilled individuals, each bringing their expertise to the table. We operated like a well-oiled machine, always one step ahead of the law.

Despite the success, there was always a part of me that felt a twinge of guilt. I justified my actions by telling myself that I was only exploiting people's greed and stupidity. But deep down, I knew I was causing real harm. The sleepless nights, the ruined lives, the desperation of my victims – it all weighed heavily on me.

The Confession

As I sit here, writing this confession, I wonder what led me to this point. Maybe it's the mounting pressure, the close calls, or perhaps it's the realization that I can't keep running forever. The life of a scammer is a lonely one, filled with mistrust and paranoia. There are no friends, only accomplices. No love, only lust. It's a hollow existence, built on lies and deceit.

This confession is my attempt to come clean, to shed light on the darkness that has consumed my life. It's a story of deception, manipulation, and the human cost of living a lie. It's my story, and I'm ready to tell it, no matter the consequences.

As I write these words, I know that the net is closing in. The authorities are closer than ever, and my luck is running out. But for the first time in years, I feel a sense of relief. The burden of my secrets is lifting, and I can finally see a glimmer of hope. This is my confession, the confession of a professional scammer.

Chapter 2: Masterpieces of Manipulation

The art of the scam is rooted in its intricacies and its ability to adapt to the mark's desires and vulnerabilities. Throughout my career, I've perfected several scams that have not only brought in significant returns but also left an indelible mark on the victims. Here, I will describe four of my most meticulously crafted scams in detail.

Scam 1: The Phantom Real Estate Deal

Target: Affluent individuals looking for lucrative investment opportunities.

Preparation: The phantom real estate deal began with a thorough study of high-value properties that were off the market but not publicly listed as sold. I'd identify properties that were either in limbo due to estate settlements or undergoing lengthy legal processes.

Execution:

1. Creating Legitimacy: I set up a sophisticated online presence for a fake real estate firm, complete with professional-looking websites, legitimate-sounding email addresses, and fake client testimonials.
2. Forging Documents: Using public records and a bit of insider knowledge, I created realistic-looking documents that showed our firm had the exclusive rights to sell these high-value properties. These documents included forged deeds, fake escrow accounts, and false title transfers.
3. Initial Contact: Through high-end networking events and exclusive online forums, I would identify potential marks. These were typically wealthy individuals or investment groups looking for prime real estate deals.
4. Building Trust: I would arrange meetings at high-end offices rented specifically for these encounters, often in well-known financial districts to add an air of legitimacy. During these meetings, I'd present the forged documents and provide a detailed portfolio of the property, complete with professional photographs and fabricated history.

5. **Closing the Deal: Once the mark was interested, I would push for a quick sale, emphasizing the exclusivity and urgency of the deal. The money would be wired to an escrow account that I controlled, under the guise of a trusted third-party escrow service.**
6. **Disappearance: After the transaction was complete, I'd vanish. The rented offices would be cleared out, the website taken down, and any trails meticulously covered.**

Outcome: The mark would only realize the scam when they attempted to take possession of the property or contact the supposed previous owners. By then, I would be long gone, having made off with millions.

Scam 2: The Charitable Foundation Fraud

Target: Philanthropists and socially conscious corporations.

Preparation: This scam involved creating a fictitious charitable foundation. I chose a cause that was currently in the public eye, ensuring it was something emotionally compelling yet slightly obscure to avoid too much scrutiny.

Execution:

1. **Building the Foundation: I established a professional-looking website for the charity,**

complete with heartfelt stories, photos of supposed beneficiaries, and testimonials from fake donors. I also created social media profiles to enhance credibility.

2. **Networking: I attended charity events, mingling with potential donors and dropping hints about the foundation's work. My team and I would even host small fundraising events to build a facade of legitimacy.**
3. **The Ask: We targeted wealthy individuals and companies known for their philanthropy. Personalized letters, phone calls, and meetings were arranged where we would present detailed plans of how their donations would make a difference. I often used fabricated success stories and data to show the charity's impact.**
4. **Donation Process: Donations were requested to be made through secure online portals linked to offshore accounts. We also encouraged the setting up of recurring donations for sustained impact.**
5. **The Switch: Once significant funds were accumulated, we slowly began siphoning money into untraceable accounts. The charity's online presence would remain active for a while to avoid suspicion.**

Outcome: By the time the donors realized the foundation was a scam, the money was already laundered through various channels. The facade was maintained just long enough to prevent immediate detection, allowing us to escape with substantial sums.

Scam 3: The Luxury Car Export Racket

Target: Car enthusiasts and small dealership owners looking for high-end vehicles at a discount.

Preparation: This scam required a deep understanding of the luxury car market and export regulations. We would identify high-demand vehicles in markets where they were scarce and overpriced.

Execution:

1. **Inventory Creation: We created fake listings for high-end vehicles on well-known car sales websites. These listings were complete with high-quality images, detailed descriptions, and attractive prices, slightly below market value to entice buyers.**
2. **Client Engagement: Interested buyers were contacted through professional email addresses and phone lines. We'd provide VIN numbers (often cloned from existing vehicles), service histories, and even virtual tours of the cars.**
3. **Secure Payments: To reassure buyers, we insisted on using secure escrow services for payment. However, these escrow services were controlled by us, giving the illusion of security while ensuring we had access to the funds.**
4. **Shipping Logistics: We arranged for the supposed shipping of these vehicles. Buyers were given tracking numbers and regular updates about the shipment's progress.**
5. **Final Act: When the delivery date approached, we'd inform the buyer of a last-minute issue – either the car was held up at customs, or there**

were unexpected shipping fees that needed immediate payment. This often led to additional payments from the buyer.

Outcome: The buyers would only realize the scam when the cars never arrived, and all communication lines went dead. By then, the escrow accounts were emptied, and any traceable evidence had been erased.

Scam 4: The High-Tech Investment Scheme

Target: Tech-savvy investors and venture capitalists looking for the next big startup.

Preparation: This scam revolved around a fictitious tech startup with a revolutionary product. We chose a cutting-edge technology, such as AI-driven financial software or a breakthrough in renewable energy, and created a believable prototype and business plan.

Execution:

1. **Company Setup:** We established a sleek, professional website and social media presence for the startup. Detailed whitepapers, patent filings (fake), and product demos (often CGI or heavily edited videos) were created to showcase the innovation.
2. **Investor Pitch:** Using platforms like AngelList and attending tech conferences, we pitched our startup to potential investors. I'd present

detailed financial projections, market analysis, and a compelling vision of the future.

3. Initial Funding Rounds: We initially sought small investments to build trust. These early investors were often paid back with interest using funds from later investors, creating a false sense of security and success.
4. Scaling Up: With a track record of successful returns, we attracted larger investors. Detailed contracts, shareholder agreements, and equity distributions were meticulously forged.
5. Exit Strategy: Once substantial funds were raised, we'd announce a major setback – perhaps a critical flaw in the technology or an insurmountable regulatory hurdle. We'd offer to buy back shares at a discounted rate to maintain credibility while siphoning the remaining funds.

Outcome: Investors were left with worthless shares in a non-existent company. By the time they realized the extent of the fraud, the money had been funneled through various shell companies and offshore accounts, making recovery impossible.

These scams required meticulous planning, a deep understanding of human psychology, and an unyielding commitment to the con. Each scheme was a dance of deception, orchestrated to perfection, leaving victims in ruins while I walked away unscathed, at least for a time. The thrill of pulling off such elaborate cons was addictive, but the stakes were always high, and the consequences of getting caught would be severe.

Chapter 2: High-Level Deceptions

Operating in the shadows of society, I've orchestrated some of the most sophisticated scams that prey on the wealthy and powerful. These high-level deceptions are meticulously planned and executed with precision, leaving victims reeling and authorities baffled. In this chapter, I will detail four of my most elaborate and successful scams, each a masterpiece of manipulation.

Scam 1: The Offshore Investment Heist

Target: Wealthy investors and corporations seeking to diversify their portfolios with offshore investments.

Preparation: The offshore investment heist required setting up an elaborate network of shell companies and offshore accounts. We chose tax havens with lax regulations, like the Cayman Islands and Panama, to base our operations.

Execution:

1. Creating the Facade: We established a professional-looking investment firm with a sleek website, high-end office spaces, and a team of well-dressed actors posing as financial advisors. The firm's portfolio included fake projects in real estate, technology, and natural resources.
2. Networking: Through exclusive investment seminars and high-profile business conferences, we mingled with potential investors. Our team portrayed an image of success and exclusivity, which attracted the attention of affluent individuals and corporations.
3. Personalized Pitches: Each potential investor received a tailored investment proposal, complete with detailed market analysis, projected returns, and risk assessments. These documents were professionally crafted to appear legitimate.
4. Securing the Funds: Investors were asked to transfer funds to secure escrow accounts for added security. These accounts were controlled by us, disguised as reputable third-party financial institutions.
5. Gradual Extraction: Instead of immediately absconding with the funds, we slowly siphoned money through various channels, maintaining the appearance of active and growing investments. This prolonged the scam and minimized suspicion.

Outcome: By the time investors realized their returns were not forthcoming, the money had been laundered through a complex web of accounts and entities. The firm's online presence vanished overnight, and our team dispersed, leaving no trace of our operation.

Scam 2: The Art Auction Racket

Target: Art collectors and wealthy individuals with a penchant for rare and valuable artworks.

Preparation: This scam involved creating fake provenance for counterfeit art pieces. We collaborated with skilled forgers who could replicate famous artists' styles to perfection.

Execution:

1. Creating the Provenance: Using forged documents, we created a history for each piece, complete with previous ownership records, auction results, and expert authentication. These documents were vital in convincing buyers of the artwork's legitimacy.
2. Setting the Stage: We rented prestigious gallery spaces in major cities and held exclusive invitation-only auctions. The ambiance, combined with expertly crafted catalogs, added an air of legitimacy.
3. Attracting the Right Crowd: Invitations were sent to known art collectors, museum curators, and high-profile individuals. We leveraged

connections in the art world to create buzz and anticipation around the auction.

4. The Auction: During the auction, professional actors posed as bidders to drive up prices. The excitement and competition encouraged real buyers to bid aggressively.
5. Finalizing the Sale: Once the winning bids were secured, buyers transferred funds to our escrow accounts. The artworks were shipped with utmost care, accompanied by the forged provenance documents.

Outcome: The scam was only uncovered when a meticulous collector or curator attempted to re authenticate the artwork. By then, the funds had been transferred through multiple offshore accounts, and the gallery's organizers had disappeared.

Scam 3: The Luxury Yacht Scam

Target: Ultra-wealthy individuals seeking to purchase or charter luxury yachts.

Preparation: We created a fictitious yacht brokerage firm, complete with an impressive fleet of high-end yachts that didn't exist. The firm's online presence was impeccable, featuring detailed specifications, high-quality images, and testimonials from satisfied clients (all fabricated).

Execution:

1. **Building the Portfolio: We used images of real yachts from various sources, altering them slightly to avoid detection. Each yacht had a detailed profile with specifications, amenities, and pricing.**
2. **Engaging Potential Clients: High-net-worth individuals were targeted through luxury lifestyle magazines, exclusive events, and personal connections. Our team portrayed themselves as elite brokers with connections to the finest yacht builders and owners.**
3. **Site Visits and Showings: Prospective buyers were invited for private showings, which were cleverly staged on rented yachts or in luxurious marina settings. We ensured the experience was convincing, with professional staff and gourmet catering.**
4. **Securing Deposits: Clients interested in purchasing or chartering a yacht were required to place significant deposits into escrow accounts. These accounts were, of course, under our control.**
5. **The Vanishing Act: After securing the deposits, we maintained communication for a while, providing updates and answering queries. Eventually, all communications ceased, and the brokerage's online presence was wiped clean.**

Outcome: By the time clients realized they had been scammed, the funds had been moved through a series of shell companies and offshore accounts. The rented office spaces were vacated, and the actors portraying our team had moved on to new identities.

Scam 4: The High-Tech Startup Con

Target: Venture capitalists and tech-savvy investors looking for the next big innovation.

Preparation: This scam required creating a fictitious tech startup with a groundbreaking product. We chose a cutting-edge field, such as artificial intelligence or blockchain technology, and developed a believable prototype and business plan.

Execution:

1. Establishing Credibility: We built a professional website, social media profiles, and press releases announcing our innovative product. We also created a team of experts (actors with impressive, fabricated resumes) to lead the company.
2. Networking and Pitching: We attended tech conferences, hackathons, and investor meetups, pitching our startup to potential investors. Our presentations were polished, backed by fabricated data and success stories.
3. Initial Funding Rounds: We secured seed funding from smaller investors, using these funds to create a semblance of progress and development. Early investors were paid returns using money from later investments, creating a false sense of success.
4. Scaling Up: With a track record of supposed success, we attracted larger investors and venture capitalists. Detailed contracts, shareholder agreements, and equity

distributions were meticulously forged to appear legitimate.

5. The Exit: Once we had amassed substantial funds, we staged a major setback, such as a critical flaw in the technology or an insurmountable regulatory hurdle. We offered to buy back shares at a discount to maintain credibility while extracting the remaining funds.

Outcome: Investors were left with worthless shares in a non-existent company. By the time they realized the extent of the fraud, the money had been laundered through various channels, making recovery impossible. The startup's online presence and the team disappeared without a trace.

These high-level scams required meticulous planning, an understanding of human psychology, and an unwavering commitment to deception. Each con was a carefully crafted masterpiece, leaving victims devastated and me one step ahead of the authorities. The thrill of executing such sophisticated scams was intoxicating, but the stakes were always high, and the consequences of getting caught would be severe.

Chapter 3: Roots in the Streets

Every master of deception has a beginning, a time when their skills were raw and unrefined, honed in the crucible of necessity and survival. Before the offshore accounts, luxury yachts, and high-tech startups, there were the streets. It was here, in the gritty underbelly of the city, that I learned the basics of the con game alongside my friends – a motley crew of street hustlers who became my family.

The Crew

Derek: The unspoken leader of our group, Derek was a tall, charismatic figure with a knack for persuasion. He could sell sand in the desert and ice in the Arctic. His silver tongue was our greatest asset, and his confidence was infectious. Derek was the one who saw potential in me and took me under his wing, teaching me the ropes.

Lenny: The muscle of the group, Lenny was built like a tank but had a surprisingly gentle demeanor. His intimidating presence often deterred trouble, and his loyalty was unwavering. Lenny was the enforcer, ensuring that deals went smoothly and that we weren't double-crossed.

Cassie: The brains behind our operations, Cassie was a tech whiz who could hack into almost anything. She had a mind for strategy and logistics, always planning three steps ahead. Her skills were invaluable in an increasingly digital world, allowing us to stay one step ahead of the authorities.

Sara: The lookout and master of disguise, Sara had a talent for blending into any environment. She could assume different personas with ease, gathering intel and slipping away unnoticed. Her sharp eyes and quick thinking often saved us from tight spots.

Together, we were a formidable team, each bringing our unique skills to the table. Our early scams were small-time but effective, laying the foundation for the more sophisticated cons that would come later.

The Fake Charity Collection

Target: Generous passersby and well-meaning citizens.

Preparation: Our first major street-level scam involved posing as charity collectors. We chose a cause that tugged at the heartstrings – helping orphaned children in war-torn countries. We created convincing flyers and donation buckets adorned with the fake charity's logo.

Execution:

1. Setting the Scene: We set up in busy areas – outside supermarkets, in shopping malls, and near tourist attractions. We dressed in matching T-shirts with the charity's name, each carrying a clipboard and a donation bucket.
2. Tugging at Heartstrings: Derek, with his persuasive charm, approached people with a heartfelt spiel about the plight of the children and how their donations could make a difference. Lenny stood nearby, his imposing presence adding an unspoken assurance of legitimacy.
3. Collecting Donations: Passersby, moved by our story and reassured by our appearance, dropped money into the buckets. Cassie and Sara moved through the crowd, subtly encouraging donations and keeping an eye out for potential trouble.
4. Switching Locations: To avoid detection, we rotated locations frequently, never staying in one spot for too long. This kept us under the radar and maximized our haul.

Outcome: By the end of each day, we had collected a significant amount of money. The scam was simple but effective, preying on people's goodwill and generosity. It was an early lesson in the power of a compelling story and a convincing appearance.

The Pigeon Drop

Target: Gullible individuals with a bit of cash to spare.

Preparation: The pigeon drop was a classic con that required careful planning and precise execution. We needed a believable story and a mark who could be convinced to part with their money.

Execution:

1. **Finding the Mark:** Sara, with her keen observational skills, identified potential marks – typically individuals who appeared to be kind-hearted but slightly naive. She would strike up a casual conversation, slowly building rapport.
2. **The Setup:** Once the mark was hooked, Sara would pretend to find a wallet or a bag filled with cash. She'd express shock and excitement, suggesting they split the money. At this point, Derek or I would join in, posing as a bystander or a concerned citizen.
3. **Creating Urgency:** Derek, with his smooth talk, would convince the mark that we needed to ensure the money wasn't stolen. He'd suggest that everyone put up some of their own money as a gesture of goodwill, to show they were trustworthy.
4. **The Drop:** The mark, eager to prove their honesty and secure their share of the found money, would hand over their cash. We'd take it, promising to meet later to split the found money and then vanish, leaving the mark empty-handed.

Outcome: The pigeon drop was a psychological play, exploiting the mark's greed and desire to appear honest. It was a delicate balance of trust and urgency, and when executed correctly, it yielded significant returns with minimal risk.

The Fake Prize Scam

Target: Shoppers and pedestrians lured by the promise of a prize.

Preparation: For this scam, we needed convincing materials – fake prize vouchers, a rented booth, and promotional materials. We chose a busy shopping district as our location.

Execution:

1. Setting Up: We set up a booth decorated with flashy banners and posters advertising a grand prize giveaway – everything from expensive electronics to vacation packages. Cassie, with her tech skills, created realistic-looking vouchers and registration forms.
2. Drawing in the Crowd: Derek, our frontman, used his charisma to draw in the crowd, promising that everyone was a potential winner. He'd explain that participants needed to register and pay a small processing fee to claim their prize.
3. Collecting Fees: Lenny managed the crowd, ensuring everything ran smoothly and handling any pushback. Sara, in various disguises, kept an eye out for law enforcement or anyone who seemed too suspicious.

4. **Disappearing Act: Once we had collected enough fees and the crowd started to thin, we'd pack up quickly and disappear before anyone could realize they'd been scammed.**

Outcome: The fake prize scam was a quick hit, capitalizing on people's desire for easy rewards. It required a bit more setup and coordination, but the returns were worth it. We learned the importance of a polished appearance and the allure of something-for-nothing.

The Fake Lottery Ticket Scam

Target: Everyday people, typically found in convenience stores and street corners.

Preparation: This scam involved creating counterfeit lottery tickets that appeared legitimate but had no real value. Cassie used her skills to replicate the tickets perfectly, ensuring they looked and felt authentic.

Execution:

1. **Creating the Tickets: Cassie's counterfeit tickets were indistinguishable from real ones. We printed a batch, ensuring some appeared to be small winners.**
2. **Approaching the Mark: Derek or I would approach someone, typically in a convenience store or on the street, and strike up a conversation. We'd casually mention that we**

had a winning lottery ticket but were in urgent need of cash and couldn't wait to cash it in ourselves.

3. Making the Swap: We'd offer to sell the "winning" ticket at a discount, convincing the mark that they were getting a great deal. The mark, thinking they were getting a guaranteed payout, would hand over cash for the ticket.
4. Vanishing Act: After the transaction, we'd disappear. By the time the mark tried to cash the ticket and discovered it was fake, we were long gone.

Outcome: The fake lottery ticket scam was a testament to the power of perceived value. It relied on the mark's excitement and haste, preventing them from scrutinizing the ticket too closely. It was a quick and effective way to make money, with minimal setup and risk.

These early street-level scams were the foundation of my education in deception. They taught me the basics of reading people, creating believable stories, and executing plans with precision. The stakes were lower, but the lessons were invaluable. Each scam, no matter how small, was a building block, preparing me for the more complex and high-stakes cons that would come later. The streets were my training ground, and my friends – Derek, Lenny, Cassie, and Sara – were my partners in crime, each one contributing to our collective success and survival.

Chapter 4: Love and Deception

In the world of scams, there is a special place for those that prey on the most vulnerable aspect of human nature: the need for love and companionship. Relationship scams, also known as romance scams, are some of the most insidious cons because they exploit deep emotions and trust. In this chapter, I will delve into the intricacies of these scams, detailing four of the most cunning and heart-wrenching cons I orchestrated.

Scam 1: The Online Romance

Target: Lonely individuals seeking love on dating websites and social media.

Preparation: To execute an online romance scam, I needed to create a convincing persona. This involved setting up fake profiles on various dating sites and social media platforms, complete with attractive photos (often stolen from unsuspecting real people) and detailed backstories.

Execution:

1. **Creating the Persona: I crafted several personas, each tailored to different demographics. One might be a successful entrepreneur, another a widowed military officer, and yet another a charming adventurer. Each profile was meticulously detailed to attract the right kind of mark.**
2. **Initial Contact: I would reach out to potential marks, sending friendly and engaging messages. The key was to establish an emotional connection quickly, making the mark feel special and understood.**
3. **Building the Relationship: Over weeks or even months, I would build a deep emotional bond with the mark. We exchanged daily messages, late-night calls, and even small gifts. I shared fabricated stories of my life, carefully mirroring the mark's interests and desires.**
4. **The Ask: Once trust and affection were established, I'd introduce a crisis. Perhaps I needed money for a medical emergency, or my business deal had fallen through, or I was stranded in a foreign country. The mark, now emotionally invested, would be eager to help.**
5. **Extraction: The mark would send money, often multiple times, believing they were helping someone they loved. Each time, I promised to repay them or meet soon, but there was always a new obstacle.**

Outcome: By the time the mark realized they had been scammed, their money was long gone, often leaving them heartbroken and financially devastated. The emotional toll was immense, making this one of the cruelest yet effective scams.

Scam 2: The Long-Distance Lover

Target: Individuals seeking serious relationships, often through international dating sites.

Preparation: For this scam, I created a persona that lived in a different country, making it easier to justify the lack of face-to-face meetings. I chose countries that were either exotic or had some inherent challenges, like political unrest or economic difficulties.

Execution:

1. **Profile Creation:** I set up profiles on international dating sites, using photos and stories that portrayed an appealing and somewhat exotic lifestyle. I often chose personas that had reasons for not being able to travel easily.
2. **Engagement:** I engaged with potential marks, showing genuine interest and affection. I used video calls sparingly, often citing poor internet connections or technical difficulties, and when I did, I used pre-recorded videos or deepfake technology to maintain the illusion.
3. **Intensifying the Relationship:** The relationship would progress quickly, with declarations of love and plans for the future. I made the mark believe that I was their soulmate, someone they were destined to be with.
4. **Visa and Travel Issues:** I would express a desire to meet but cite issues like visa

problems, legal troubles, or financial constraints. I'd ask for money to resolve these issues, promising to pay it back once we were together.

5. Milking the Situation: Each request for money came with a heartfelt plea and a plausible excuse. I'd assure the mark that we were close to solving the problem and being together, only to introduce new hurdles.

Outcome: The mark, driven by love and the hope of a future together, would send money repeatedly. When they finally realized they had been conned, the emotional and financial damage was significant, leaving them disillusioned and wary of future relationships.

Scam 3: The Fake Marriage Proposal

Target: Individuals desperate for marriage, often through matrimonial websites or cultural-specific dating platforms.

Preparation: This scam required a persona that appeared sincere and committed to marriage. I targeted matrimonial websites and cultural-specific dating platforms where individuals were specifically looking for long-term commitments.

Execution:

1. Profile Creation: I created profiles that reflected stability and seriousness. My personas

included successful professionals, devout individuals, or those with strong family values, depending on the target demographic.

2. **Courtship: I courted potential marks with an air of seriousness, discussing marriage, family values, and future plans early on. I tailored my approach to align with the cultural or religious expectations of the mark.**
3. **Meeting the Family: I'd arrange virtual meetings with the mark's family, often involving my own "family" (played by accomplices) to add legitimacy. These meetings were key to building trust and commitment.**
4. **Engagement Expenses: After a period of courtship, I'd propose marriage. The mark, now deeply invested, would eagerly agree. I'd then introduce expenses related to the engagement or wedding – such as purchasing a ring, booking venues, or covering traditional ceremonies.**
5. **Final Push: As the supposed wedding date approached, I'd escalate the financial demands, citing last-minute emergencies or additional costs. The mark, caught up in the excitement and anticipation, would continue to send money.**

Outcome: The scam culminated in the mark sending large sums of money for a wedding that would never happen. When the truth finally surfaced, the emotional devastation was profound, often leaving the victim with deep trust issues and financial hardships.

Scam 4: The Inheritance Heir

Target: Wealthy individuals or those with access to significant funds, usually found through social media or high-end dating platforms.

Preparation: For the inheritance heir scam, I created a persona of someone from a wealthy background who stood to inherit a substantial fortune but needed help accessing it. This involved crafting a backstory of family feuds, legal battles, or complicated financial situations.

Execution:

1. Profile Creation: I developed a profile that exuded wealth and sophistication. My persona would often be someone who was currently facing difficulties accessing their inheritance due to legal or bureaucratic hurdles.
2. Building the Connection: I'd engage with potential marks, sharing stories of my lavish lifestyle and the struggles of dealing with greedy relatives or corrupt officials. The marks were drawn in by the allure of wealth and the excitement of a dramatic story.
3. Emotional Bond: I'd build a strong emotional connection, sharing personal stories and expressing a deep need for support. The mark would feel special, chosen to help in this critical time.
4. The Inheritance Issue: Once the relationship was strong, I'd introduce the main issue – needing money to pay for legal fees, bribes, or other expenses to unlock the inheritance. The

mark, now emotionally invested, would be eager to help.

5. **Continuous Requests: Each time the mark sent money, I'd introduce a new problem, ensuring the requests seemed plausible and necessary. The mark believed they were close to a huge payday, motivating them to keep sending funds.**

Outcome: The mark would be left waiting for an inheritance that would never materialize. By the time they realized they had been scammed, their financial and emotional losses were substantial. The elaborate story and strong emotional bond made it difficult for them to accept the truth.

Relationship scams are particularly cruel because they exploit the fundamental human need for connection and affection. Each scam I executed required not just a convincing story, but an ability to manipulate emotions and build deep trust. The marks were not just victims of financial fraud; they were victims of heartbreak and betrayal, making these scams some of the most devastating. The allure of love, the promise of companionship, and the hope of a better future were powerful tools in my arsenal, turning dreams into nightmares and leaving a trail of broken hearts in my wake.

Chapter 5: The Voice of Deception

The power of a persuasive voice cannot be underestimated, especially when it comes to phone scams. These scams capitalize on the immediacy and intimacy of a phone call, exploiting the trust people place in a direct conversation. Over the years, I perfected various phone sales scams, each tailored to manipulate and defraud the unsuspecting. In this chapter, I'll detail four of the most effective and lucrative phone sales scams I orchestrated.

Scam 1: The Fake Tech Support Call

Target: Elderly individuals and less tech-savvy people.

Preparation: For the fake tech support scam, I needed a list of potential marks, typically sourced from data breaches or purchased from shady vendors. These lists often included basic personal information like names, phone numbers, and sometimes even email addresses.

Execution:

1. Initial Contact: I'd call the mark, posing as a representative from a well-known tech company like Microsoft or Apple. My tone was

professional and reassuring, designed to instill trust from the start.

2. The Problem: I'd inform the mark that their computer had been flagged for malware or suspicious activity. This usually elicited immediate concern, especially from those less familiar with technology.
3. Gaining Access: I'd guide the mark through the process of granting me remote access to their computer, under the guise of diagnosing and fixing the problem. With remote access, I could manipulate their system to display fake error messages and logs.
4. The Solution: After "diagnosing" the issue, I'd offer a solution – a one-time fix for a fee or, more lucratively, a subscription to ongoing tech support services. The fees varied but were always positioned as a necessary expense to protect their data and privacy.
5. Payment: I'd direct the mark to a secure payment page (created by me) to enter their credit card details. Alternatively, I'd ask for payment through gift cards, which were harder to trace and easier to liquidate.

Outcome: By the time the mark realized there was no real problem, they had already paid for unnecessary services. The scam capitalized on fear and the victim's lack of technical knowledge, making it highly effective and difficult to trace.

Scam 2: The Telemarketing Charity Fraud

Target: Generous individuals and small business owners.

Preparation: Creating a convincing charity required setting up a fake organization complete with a website, fake testimonials, and a list of potential marks. We focused on causes that resonated deeply with people, such as helping veterans, children, or disaster relief.

Execution:

1. **Initial Call:** I'd call potential donors, introducing myself as a representative of the charity. My pitch was heartfelt and urgent, often citing a recent event or an ongoing crisis that needed immediate funds.
2. **Building Trust:** I'd provide a brief overview of the charity's mission, citing fake statistics and success stories. I'd direct them to the charity's professional-looking website if they wanted to verify its legitimacy.
3. **The Ask:** I'd ask for a donation, explaining how even a small amount could make a big difference. For larger businesses, I'd suggest a more substantial donation, offering recognition on our website or at charity events.
4. **Closing the Deal:** Once the mark agreed to donate, I'd direct them to provide their payment information over the phone or send them a secure link to complete the donation online.
5. **Follow-Up:** To maintain the facade, I'd send a thank-you email with a receipt and

occasionally follow up with newsletters or updates on the charity's "progress."

Outcome: The donations would pour in, and by the time anyone suspected foul play, the charity's online presence would vanish, along with the funds. The emotional appeal of helping those in need made this scam particularly effective.

Scam 3: The Extended Warranty Scam

Target: Car owners, particularly those with older vehicles.

Preparation: For the extended warranty scam, I sourced lists of car owners from public records and databases. The marks typically owned vehicles that were out of warranty, making them prime targets for this con.

Execution:

1. Initial Contact: I'd call the mark, posing as a representative from a well-known car manufacturer or a reputable warranty company. I'd inform them that their vehicle's warranty was about to expire or had already expired.
2. The Pitch: I'd explain the benefits of an extended warranty, emphasizing potential repair costs and the peace of mind that comes with coverage. My pitch was designed to create a sense of urgency and necessity.

3. Pricing Options: I'd offer various warranty packages, each with different levels of coverage and pricing. The goal was to make at least one option seem affordable and essential.
4. Payment: Once the mark chose a package, I'd collect their payment information over the phone. Alternatively, I'd direct them to a secure payment portal (controlled by me) to enter their details.
5. Confirmation: I'd send a confirmation email with fake warranty documents and contact information for "customer service," maintaining the illusion of legitimacy.

Outcome: The mark believed they had purchased valuable protection for their vehicle, only to find out later that the warranty was worthless when they tried to make a claim. By then, the funds were long gone, and the fake company had disappeared.

Scam 4: The Prize Notification Scam

Target: Individuals excited by the prospect of winning prizes or sweepstakes.

Preparation: For this scam, I used data from online sweepstakes entries and consumer surveys. These sources provided lists of people who frequently entered contests and were likely to believe they had won a prize.

Execution:

1. Initial Call: I'd call the mark, congratulating them on winning a significant prize – often cash, a vacation, or a luxury item. The excitement in my voice was contagious, designed to elicit a positive response.
2. Verifying Information: I'd ask the mark to verify their information, including their name, address, and sometimes even financial details, under the guise of confirming their identity.
3. Claiming the Prize: I'd explain that to claim their prize, they needed to pay a small processing fee or taxes upfront. This fee was always positioned as a minor expense compared to the value of the prize.
4. Payment Collection: I'd collect the payment over the phone or direct them to a secure payment page. In some cases, I'd ask for payment via gift cards or wire transfers to make the funds harder to trace.
5. False Assurance: To keep the scam going, I'd send a follow-up email with details about the prize delivery, sometimes even providing fake tracking numbers or delivery dates.

Outcome: The mark would be eagerly awaiting their prize, only to receive nothing. By the time they realized the scam, their money was gone, and any attempt to contact the prize company led to dead ends. The allure of a big win blinded them to the red flags.

Phone sales scams are a testament to the power of a persuasive voice and a well-crafted story. Each scam relied on creating a sense of urgency and trust, exploiting the marks' fears, desires, and generosity. The direct, personal nature of a phone call made these scams highly effective, often leaving victims with empty pockets and shattered trust. The anonymity of a phone call, combined with the ability to disappear without a trace, made these scams some of the most lucrative and difficult to track. The art of deception thrives on human vulnerability, and there is no better tool to exploit it than the simple telephone.

Chapter 6: The Hospital Hustle

In the shadowy world of scams, some con artists prey on the vulnerabilities within institutions meant to protect and heal. The hospital scam to obtain drugs is one such scheme, exploiting the very systems designed to safeguard public health. This chapter delves into the intricate details of how I orchestrated a hospital scam to acquire prescription drugs, a con that required meticulous planning, persuasive skills, and a deep understanding of medical procedures.

The Setup

Target: Hospitals and clinics with stringent but sometimes overburdened systems for dispensing prescription drugs.

Preparation: The success of this scam hinged on creating a convincing backstory and persona. I needed to appear as a legitimate patient with a credible medical history that warranted the prescription of controlled substances. This involved creating fake medical records, learning medical jargon, and understanding the symptoms of the conditions I was feigning.

Execution:

1. Creating a Medical History:
    - Fake Documents: I crafted fake medical records, complete with detailed histories of chronic pain or other conditions that required strong painkillers. These documents included notes from fake doctors, diagnostic test results, and previous prescriptions.
    - Online Research: I researched medical conditions extensively, learning the symptoms and treatment protocols to convincingly portray a patient in need.
2. Choosing the Hospital:
    - Target Selection: I selected hospitals and clinics that were busy and had high patient turnover, making it easier to slip through the cracks. I avoided facilities with overly stringent verification processes.

- Initial Visit: I made an initial visit to scout the hospital, noting the layout, security measures, and staff routines.

3. The Visit:
   - Appearance and Demeanor: On the day of the visit, I dressed appropriately and adopted the demeanor of someone in severe pain but trying to remain composed. The goal was to elicit sympathy and prompt action from the medical staff.
   - Registration: At the reception, I provided the fake medical records and answered questions confidently. I used an alias to avoid linking the scam back to my real identity.
   - Symptoms Presentation: During the consultation, I described my symptoms in detail, mimicking the pain and discomfort associated with my fabricated condition. I used medical terminology to add authenticity and referenced the fake records to support my claims.
4. Convincing the Doctor:
   - Emotional Appeal: I made an emotional appeal, emphasizing the impact of the pain on my daily life and my desperate need for relief. I expressed frustration at previous treatments and hinted at worsening symptoms.
   - Requesting Specific Medications: Based on my research, I knew which drugs were commonly prescribed for my supposed condition. I subtly steered the conversation towards these medications,

suggesting that they had been effective in the past.

5. Prescription and Dispensation:
    - Prescription Issued: If the doctor was convinced, they would write a prescription for the desired medication. In some cases, I was referred to a specialist, but I usually managed to get at least a short-term prescription.
    - Pharmacy Visit: I took the prescription to the hospital's pharmacy or a nearby pharmacy, ensuring it was filled without raising suspicion. I often used different pharmacies to avoid detection.

Outcome: The scam was successful if the prescription was filled without incident, providing me with the desired drugs. The frequency and location of these visits had to be carefully managed to avoid patterns that could lead to suspicion or investigation. Each successful visit added to my stockpile, which could be used personally or sold on the black market.

The Risks and Ethical Dilemmas

While this scam was lucrative, it was fraught with risks and ethical dilemmas. The consequences of getting caught were severe, including legal action and imprisonment. Moreover, exploiting the healthcare system and manipulating medical professionals felt deeply unethical, even for a seasoned scammer like me. The potential harm to real patients, the strain on already overburdened healthcare workers, and the contribution to the illegal drug trade were significant moral burdens.

Evolving the Scam

As healthcare systems became more vigilant and technology advanced, the hospital scam needed constant adaptation. Electronic medical records, stricter verification processes, and increased awareness of prescription drug abuse made the con more challenging. Here's how I evolved the scam:

1. Digital Manipulation:
    - Hacking Skills: Cassie, our tech whiz, hacked into medical databases to create more convincing digital records. This allowed for seamless integration of fake histories into real systems.
    - Telemedicine Exploits: With the rise of telemedicine, I exploited the less stringent remote consultations. Posing as a patient over video calls was often easier than in-person visits.
2. Network Expansion:
    - Accomplices: I recruited accomplices to act as patients, diversifying the identities and stories used in the scam. This reduced the risk of detection and allowed for more frequent visits.
    - Insider Information: I cultivated relationships with insiders within hospitals and pharmacies who provided tips on when and where to strike.
3. Sophisticated Cover Stories:

- Complex Histories: My backstories became more complex and layered, with multiple conditions and treatment attempts. This made the fake histories more believable and harder to debunk.
- Real Symptoms: Occasionally, I induced minor symptoms that matched the conditions I was faking, such as inflammation or bruising, to make the presentation more convincing.

Outcome: These adaptations allowed the scam to continue operating despite increased scrutiny. However, the risks remained high, and the ethical toll grew heavier with each passing day.

The hospital scam to obtain drugs was a dark chapter in my career, highlighting the lengths to which deception could be taken. It was a con that exploited both the compassion of healthcare professionals and the vulnerabilities of the system. While it brought significant rewards, it also carried immense risks and moral consequences. This scam was a stark reminder that in the world of cons, even the most sophisticated schemes come at a price, both legally and ethically.

Chapter 7: The Service Provider Scam

The service provider scam is a particularly insidious form of fraud, exploiting trust and necessity in the realm of essential services. It involves posing as legitimate service providers—such as utility companies, internet providers, or repair technicians—to extract money from unsuspecting victims. This chapter delves into the intricacies of these scams, detailing the preparation, execution, and aftermath of four particularly effective schemes.

Scam 1: The Utility Bill Fraud

Target: Homeowners and renters, particularly those less tech-savvy or with a history of late payments.

Preparation: To execute the utility bill fraud, I needed access to information about utility account holders, such as names, addresses, and account details. This information was often obtained through data breaches or purchased from underground markets.

Execution:

1. Creating the Caller ID:
    - Spoofing Technology: Using caller ID spoofing technology, I made it appear as though the call was coming from a legitimate utility company. This added an air of authenticity right from the start.
2. The Initial Call:
    - Professional Tone: I called the mark, posing as a representative from their

utility company. My tone was professional, and I had a script that mirrored the standard customer service protocols.
    - **Urgent Issue:** I informed the mark of an urgent issue with their account, such as an overdue bill or a problem that required immediate payment to avoid service disruption.
3. **Payment Demand:**
    - **Threat of Disconnection:** I emphasized the consequences of non-payment, such as immediate disconnection of services. This created a sense of urgency and panic.
    - **Payment Method:** I directed the mark to pay immediately via a secure payment link or over the phone. Often, I suggested methods that were harder to trace, like prepaid debit cards or wire transfers.
4. **Confirmation:**
    - **Fake Confirmation Number:** After receiving the payment, I provided a fake confirmation number to give the mark a sense of security and closure.

Outcome: By the time the mark realized their payment was not registered with their actual utility company, the money had already been transferred and laundered through various channels. The fear of losing essential services made this scam particularly effective.

Scam 2: The Internet Service Upgrade

Target: Internet service subscribers, especially those in areas with limited provider options.

Preparation: This scam required knowledge of the local internet service providers (ISPs) and their customer base. I created a list of potential marks using publicly available information and previous data breaches.

Execution:

1. Initial Contact:
   - Spoofing Caller ID: As with the utility scam, I used caller ID spoofing to make it appear as though the call was coming from a legitimate ISP.
   - Offer of Upgrade: I called the mark, introducing myself as a representative from their ISP. I offered a limited-time upgrade to a faster internet plan at a discounted rate, emphasizing the improved speed and reliability.
2. Creating Urgency:
   - Limited-Time Offer: I stressed that the offer was only available for a short period, creating a sense of urgency. This pressured the mark into making a quick decision.
   - Immediate Payment Required: To secure the upgrade, I required immediate payment. I offered to take the payment over the phone or through a secure link.
3. Payment Processing:

    - Collecting Payment: The mark would provide their payment details, which I processed through a fake payment gateway. I assured them they would see the upgrade reflected in their next billing cycle.

4. Follow-Up:
    - Fake Confirmation: I sent a follow-up email with a fake confirmation of the upgrade, complete with details of the new plan and the next billing date.

Outcome: The mark would only realize they had been scammed when they saw no change in their internet service or billing. By then, the payment had been funneled through multiple accounts, making it difficult to trace.

Scam 3: The Home Repair Racket

Target: Homeowners, particularly the elderly and those living in older homes.

Preparation: This scam involved posing as a contractor or home repair technician. I needed to create a convincing business front, complete with a website, business cards, and references (all fabricated).

Execution:

1. Initial Contact:

- Cold Calls: I made cold calls to homeowners, offering free home inspections or discounted repair services. My targets were typically those who had older homes or lived in areas known for home maintenance issues.

2. Inspection and Diagnosis:
    - Fake Inspection: During the free inspection, I would "discover" critical issues that required immediate attention. These problems were either fabricated or exaggerated, playing on the homeowner's fears of structural damage or safety hazards.
    - Detailed Report: I provided a detailed report with alarming findings and high repair estimates, often using technical jargon to make the issues seem more severe.
3. Securing Payment:
    - Urgent Repairs: I stressed the urgency of the repairs, offering to start work immediately for a deposit or full upfront payment. I provided a contract that appeared legitimate but was filled with vague terms and conditions.
    - Collecting Funds: The homeowner would provide payment, either by check, credit card, or cash. I assured them that work would begin the next day.
4. Disappearing Act:
    - Vanishing: After receiving payment, I would disappear, leaving the homeowner with unfinished or shoddy repairs. In some cases, I did no work at all, simply taking the money and running.

Outcome: Homeowners would be left with unresolved issues and out significant amounts of money. By the time they attempted to contact the business, the phone lines were disconnected, and the website was taken down.

Scam 4: The Tech Support Subscription

Target: Individuals with limited tech knowledge, often the elderly or those working from home.

Preparation: For the tech support subscription scam, I created a fake tech support company with a professional-looking website and advertisements. These ads were placed on popular websites and search engines to attract potential marks.

Execution:

1. Initial Contact:
    - Online Ads: Potential marks would see ads offering comprehensive tech support subscriptions at attractive rates. The ads promised 24/7 support, virus protection, and regular system maintenance.
    - Phone Call or Chat: Interested individuals were directed to call a toll-free number or initiate a chat on the website. I'd answer these calls or chats, posing as a tech support specialist.
2. Subscription Plan:
    - Explaining Benefits: I explained the benefits of the subscription, using

technical jargon to impress and convince the mark of the service's value. The plan often included features that seemed essential for modern tech use.
   - Immediate Sign-Up: I offered a discounted rate for immediate sign-up, creating urgency by stating it was a limited-time offer.
3. Payment Processing:
   - Collecting Payment: The mark would provide their payment details over the phone or through the website's payment portal. I assured them that they would receive immediate access to the support services.
   - Confirmation Email: After processing the payment, I sent a confirmation email with login details and instructions on how to access the support services.
4. Non-Existent Support:
   - Lack of Service: When the mark attempted to use the support services, they either found them non-functional or faced long wait times and unhelpful responses. Eventually, the support lines would go dead, and the website would be taken down.

Outcome: Victims were left without the tech support they paid for, often realizing too late that they had been scammed. The funds were quickly transferred through various accounts, leaving little trace for authorities to follow.

The service provider scam is a prime example of how trust and necessity can be exploited for financial gain. Each of these scams relied on creating a sense of urgency and legitimacy, making it difficult for the marks to see through the deception. By the time they realized they had been conned, the money was already gone, leaving them not only out of pocket but also wary and distrustful of genuine service providers in the future. The voice on the other end of the line, combined with a well-crafted story, proved to be a powerful tool in the arsenal of deception.

Chapter 8: The Prepaid Credit Card Scam

The prepaid credit card scam is a sophisticated con that preys on people's trust and lack of familiarity with financial processes. By manipulating victims into purchasing and sharing the details of prepaid credit cards, scammers can quickly and effectively steal funds with little risk of being traced. This chapter explores the intricate details of how I orchestrated one of my most successful prepaid credit card scams, from preparation to execution, and the eventual aftermath.

The Setup

Target: Individuals unfamiliar with prepaid credit cards, often found through social media, job boards, or random cold calls.

Preparation: Executing this scam required a deep understanding of prepaid credit card systems and creating a convincing cover story. I needed a list of potential marks, often obtained through data breaches or purchased from illicit sources. The scam also necessitated creating fake business fronts and websites to add credibility.

Execution

1. Creating the Cover Story

- Fake Businesses: I set up websites for fake businesses, such as online marketplaces, tech support services, or mystery shopping companies. These websites were professionally designed, complete with customer testimonials, product listings, and contact information.
- Social Media Presence: I created social media profiles for these businesses, posting regularly to build a semblance of legitimacy. Ads and posts were designed to attract potential marks, often promising easy money or free services.

2. Initial Contact

- Cold Calls and Emails: I contacted potential marks through cold calls, emails, and social media messages. The pitch varied depending on the business front. For the tech support scam, I warned of urgent computer issues. For the mystery shopping scam, I offered lucrative assignments that required upfront costs.

- **Building Trust:** During these initial contacts, I used professional language and provided references to the fake business websites and social media profiles. This built trust and reassured the marks that they were dealing with a legitimate entity.

3. The Ask

- **Urgency and Pressure:** I created a sense of urgency, claiming that the offer or problem required immediate action. For example, a tech support scam might involve a fake virus that needed instant removal, while a mystery shopping scam could involve a limited-time offer.
- **Request for Prepaid Cards:** I explained that the best way to resolve the issue or secure the offer was through prepaid credit cards. I claimed this method was secure and quick. I instructed the marks to purchase prepaid cards from a local store and share the card details over the phone or through a secure form on the website.

4. Collection of Card Details

- **Receiving Information:** Once the mark purchased the prepaid cards, they would provide the card numbers and security codes, believing this was necessary to complete the transaction or service.

- Immediate Usage: As soon as I received the card details, I quickly used the funds for online purchases, transferred the balance to other accounts, or sold the card information on the dark web.

5. Final Assurance

- Confirmation: After receiving the card details, I sent a confirmation email or message, assuring the mark that the issue was resolved or the offer was secured. This delayed their suspicion and gave me more time to use the funds.

Detailed Case Studies

Case Study 1: The Tech Support Crisis

Target: Elderly individuals with limited tech knowledge.

Execution:

1. Initial Contact: I called the mark, posing as a representative from a well-known tech company. I informed them that their computer was infected with a dangerous virus that could steal their personal information.
2. Urgent Solution: I explained that immediate action was needed to prevent data loss and identity theft. I recommended purchasing a

prepaid credit card to cover the cost of an emergency security software installation.

3. **Collection and Usage:** The mark purchased the card and provided the details. I assured them that the software would be installed remotely and their computer was now safe. The card funds were quickly used for online purchases before the mark realized there was no actual software.

Outcome: The elderly mark was left out of pocket, believing they had protected their computer. The scam relied on their fear and lack of technical knowledge.

Case Study 2: The Mystery Shopper Opportunity

Target: Job seekers looking for easy, flexible work.

Execution:

1. **Initial Contact:** I posted ads on job boards and social media, offering high-paying mystery shopper assignments. Interested individuals were directed to a professional-looking website to sign up.
2. **Assignment Offer:** I contacted the applicants, explaining that they had been selected for a prestigious assignment. To proceed, they needed to purchase items using prepaid credit cards to test the payment process.
3. **Collection and Usage:** Applicants bought the cards and provided the details, believing they

would be reimbursed and paid for their time. I quickly used the card funds, leaving the marks waiting for payments that would never come.

Outcome: Job seekers, eager for work, were left without the promised reimbursements and pay. The scam exploited their need for employment and trust in the mystery shopping process.

Case Study 3: The Charity Donation

Target: Generous individuals wanting to contribute to a good cause.

Execution:

1. **Initial Contact: I sent emails and social media messages posing as a representative from a reputable charity, claiming an urgent need for funds due to a natural disaster.**
2. **Donation Request: I explained that the fastest way to send support was through prepaid credit cards, citing logistical reasons and promising that every cent would go directly to those in need.**
3. **Collection and Usage: Donors purchased the cards and provided the details, believing they were making a real difference. The funds were swiftly transferred and used for personal gain.**

Outcome: Generous individuals, motivated by a desire to help, were defrauded. The scam took advantage of their goodwill and the urgency of a fabricated crisis.

Aftermath and Evolution

As with all scams, the prepaid credit card con had to evolve with changing technology and increased awareness. Here's how I adapted the scam:

1. Advanced Spoofing: Improved caller ID spoofing techniques made the initial contact appear even more legitimate.
2. Better Websites: Enhanced website design and social media integration added more layers of credibility.
3. Multiple Fronts: Diversifying the types of scams (tech support, mystery shopping, charity) allowed for broader reach and minimized the risk of detection.

Risks and Ethical Considerations

The prepaid credit card scam, while lucrative, carried significant risks. The legal consequences of getting caught were severe, and the emotional toll on victims was substantial. Exploiting trust and urgency made the scam particularly cruel, and the ethical implications weighed heavily, even for a seasoned scammer like me.

The prepaid credit card scam is a stark example of how deception can exploit trust and necessity. By understanding and manipulating human psychology, these scams extract funds quickly and efficiently, leaving victims with financial losses and emotional scars. The evolution of technology and the constant need for new tactics highlight the ever-changing landscape of fraud. While the rewards were significant, the risks and ethical costs were always looming, reminding me that in the world of scams, every gain comes at a price.

Chapter 9: The Cartel Kidnapping Scam

The cartel kidnapping scam is one of the most terrifying and psychologically manipulative cons in the world of crime. This scam preys on fear and the instinctive urge to protect loved ones. By creating the illusion of a kidnapping orchestrated by a dangerous cartel, scammers can extort significant sums of money from their victims. In this chapter, I will detail the meticulous planning, execution, and aftermath of the cartel kidnapping scam.

The Setup

Target: Wealthy individuals, business owners, and families with significant assets.

Preparation: Executing a convincing cartel kidnapping scam required extensive research on the targets, understanding their routines, and crafting a plausible scenario. This involved gathering personal information through social media, public records, and other sources.

Execution

1. Research and Selection

- **Identifying Targets:** I used social media, local news, and business directories to identify potential targets with significant assets and a public presence. I looked for individuals with visible wealth and active social lives.
- **Gathering Information:** Detailed information about the targets' families, daily routines, and travel plans was collected. This included names, addresses, phone numbers, and any personal details that could be used to enhance the believability of the scam.

2. Creating the Scenario

- **Crafting the Story:** I crafted a detailed script that would be used during the scam. The story involved the "kidnapping" of a family member by a ruthless cartel demanding a ransom. The script included specific threats, detailed descriptions of the supposed kidnapping, and instructions for the ransom payment.
- **Setting the Scene:** To make the scam more believable, I ensured the timing of the call

coincided with the target's inability to immediately verify the safety of their loved ones (e.g., during travel, at work, or late at night).

3. The Initial Call

- Voice Manipulation: Using voice modulation technology, I altered my voice to sound menacing and foreign, enhancing the credibility of the cartel threat.
- Immediate Fear: The initial call was made to the target, typically the parent or spouse of the supposed kidnapping victim. I began with a sense of urgency and fear, stating that their loved one had been kidnapped by a cartel.
- Detailed Threats: I provided specific details about the loved one's appearance, daily routine, and recent activities to make the threat more credible. I described gruesome consequences if the ransom was not paid quickly.

4. Negotiation and Payment

- Ransom Demand: A significant ransom was demanded, often in the form of untraceable payment methods such as cryptocurrency or wire transfers to offshore accounts. I emphasized the need for secrecy and immediate action to ensure the victim's safety.
- Creating Urgency: I used psychological manipulation to create a sense of urgency and prevent the target from contacting authorities. Statements like "any delay will cost your loved one's life" were common.

- Guided Payment: I guided the target through the payment process, ensuring they had no time to verify the situation. This included detailed instructions on how to transfer funds and threats to keep them compliant.

5. Resolution and Vanishing

- Releasing the "Victim": After the ransom was paid, I assured the target that their loved one would be released shortly. I then vanished, cutting off all communication and leaving the target in a state of relief mixed with lingering fear.
- Covering Tracks: The ransom money was quickly laundered through a network of accounts and cryptocurrency transactions, making it difficult to trace. Any digital footprints were meticulously erased to avoid detection.

Detailed Case Study

Target: A wealthy business owner with a high public profile.

Execution:

1. Initial Research: I identified Mr. Thompson, a wealthy business owner known for his philanthropy and frequent public appearances. Detailed information about his family and

routines was gathered from social media and public records.

2. Crafting the Story: The script involved the kidnapping of his daughter, who was a university student. I included specific details about her recent activities, classes, and friends to enhance believability.
3. Initial Call: Using a voice modulator, I called Mr. Thompson late at night, knowing he would be less likely to verify his daughter's safety immediately. I claimed that a cartel had kidnapped his daughter and demanded a ransom of $500,000.
4. Creating Urgency: I described in gruesome detail the consequences of not paying the ransom immediately. I instructed Mr. Thompson to withdraw the money and transfer it to a cryptocurrency wallet within two hours, emphasizing secrecy.
5. Payment: Mr. Thompson, driven by fear and urgency, followed the instructions and transferred the money. I assured him that his daughter would be released shortly and then cut off all communication.
6. Aftermath: Mr. Thompson discovered the scam only after contacting his daughter, who was safe and unaware of the situation. By then, the money had been laundered through a series of transactions, making it nearly impossible to recover.

Risks and Ethical Considerations

The cartel kidnapping scam, while highly effective, carried immense risks. The psychological toll on the victims was severe, and the legal consequences of getting caught included lengthy imprisonment. Moreover, the ethical implications were profound. Exploiting a person's love and fear for their family is one of the most morally reprehensible acts, even in the world of cons.

Evolution and Adaptation

As awareness of such scams grew, the methods had to evolve. Here's how the scam was adapted over time:

1. Enhanced Technology: Using more sophisticated voice modulation and call spoofing technology to make the calls appear even more credible.
2. Diversified Targets: Expanding the target pool to include not just wealthy individuals but also middle-class families, increasing the frequency of successful scams.
3. Psychological Tactics: Employing psychological experts to refine the scripts and enhance the emotional manipulation techniques used during the calls.
4. Real-Time Monitoring: Monitoring the target's social media in real-time during the scam to incorporate up-to-the-minute details and increase believability.

Conclusion

The cartel kidnapping scam is a dark testament to the power of fear and love. By exploiting these powerful emotions, scammers can extract significant sums of money with relative ease. However, the human cost is immense, leaving victims traumatized and financially devastated. While the rewards were substantial, the risks and ethical implications made this one of the most challenging and morally troubling scams in my career. In the end, it served as a reminder that even in the world of deception, some lines are perhaps too dark to cross without leaving a permanent mark on the soul.

Chapter 10: The Blind Eye of Justice

One of the most perplexing and frustrating aspects of the world of scamming is the apparent indifference of law enforcement to the plight of scam victims. Despite the significant financial and emotional toll these crimes inflict, many scammers operate with a surprising degree of impunity. In this chapter, I explore the reasons behind law enforcement's seeming lack of concern about scammers, shedding light on the complexities and challenges of policing this shadowy world.

The Scale of the Problem

1. The Sheer Volume: Scams are pervasive, affecting millions of people across the globe. The sheer number of scams, ranging from small-time cons to elaborate international schemes, overwhelms law enforcement agencies. With limited resources, it becomes nearly impossible to investigate and prosecute every case.

2. Low Priority: Compared to violent crimes like murder, assault, or terrorism, scams are often seen as less urgent. Law enforcement agencies prioritize crimes that pose an immediate threat to physical safety over financial fraud, which, while damaging, is viewed as less critical.

The Complexity of Scams

1. Technological Sophistication: Modern scams often involve sophisticated technology, including phishing, hacking, and spoofing techniques. Law enforcement agencies may lack the technical expertise or resources to track and combat these high-tech crimes effectively.

2. Jurisdictional Challenges: Many scams are perpetrated by international syndicates, with perpetrators operating from countries with weak or non-cooperative law enforcement. Jurisdictional issues make it difficult to pursue and prosecute scammers who operate across borders.

3. Lack of Physical Evidence: Scams often leave little physical evidence. Transactions are conducted electronically, identities are fabricated, and digital footprints are easily erased. Without tangible

evidence, building a case becomes exceedingly difficult.

Victim Reluctance

1. Shame and Embarrassment: Many victims of scams feel ashamed or embarrassed about being deceived. They may be reluctant to report the crime, fearing judgment or ridicule. This underreporting leads to a lack of data and urgency from law enforcement.

2. Small Financial Losses: While some scams result in significant financial losses, many involve relatively small amounts of money. Victims may not see the point in reporting smaller losses, believing that law enforcement won't prioritize their case.

Resource Constraints

1. Limited Manpower: Law enforcement agencies are often understaffed and overburdened. Officers are stretched thin, handling a wide range of criminal activities. Financial fraud units, where they exist, are usually small and under-resourced.

2. Budget Limitations: Investigating scams, especially those involving complex technology or international elements, requires significant financial resources. Budget constraints mean that many agencies cannot afford to allocate the necessary funds to pursue these cases aggressively.

Legal Hurdles

1. Burden of Proof: Prosecuting a scammer requires a high burden of proof. Law enforcement must demonstrate not only that a crime occurred but that the accused had the intent to defraud. This can be particularly challenging in cases where scammers use sophisticated methods to cover their tracks.

2. Slow Legal Processes: Even when scammers are identified and apprehended, the legal process can be slow and cumbersome. Gathering evidence, filing charges, and going to trial can take years, during which time the scammer may continue their activities.

Public Perception and Policy

1. Misconceptions About Victims: There is a pervasive misconception that scam victims are gullible or naive. This societal attitude can influence law enforcement's approach, leading to a lack of empathy and urgency in addressing these crimes.

2. Inadequate Legislation: Laws regarding financial fraud and cybercrime often lag behind the rapidly evolving tactics of scammers. Inadequate or outdated legislation can hinder law enforcement's ability to effectively pursue and prosecute these crimes.

The Scammer's Perspective

From the perspective of a scammer, law enforcement's challenges and limitations create a fertile ground for continued operations. Understanding these weaknesses allows scammers to exploit the system, adapting their methods to avoid detection and prosecution.

1. Low Risk, High Reward: The perception that scamming carries a low risk of apprehension and prosecution, combined with potentially high financial rewards, incentivizes continued criminal activity.

2. Adaptability: Scammers are highly adaptable, constantly evolving their techniques to stay ahead of law enforcement. They monitor changes in legislation and law enforcement tactics, adjusting their operations accordingly.

Conclusion

Law enforcement's seeming indifference to scammers is a complex issue rooted in resource limitations, technological challenges, jurisdictional hurdles, and societal attitudes. While individual officers and agencies may care deeply about combating financial fraud, the systemic obstacles they face often render their efforts insufficient. For victims, this reality can be disheartening, reinforcing the need for greater awareness, better resources, and more robust legal frameworks to tackle the ever-evolving world of scams. In the end, addressing these crimes requires a concerted effort from law enforcement, policymakers, and society as a whole to better protect individuals from the predators lurking in the shadows.

Chapter 11: The Anatomy of a Scammer

Scammers come in many shapes and forms, but those who excel in the art of deception share certain traits and skills that set them apart from the rest. In this chapter, I will explore the qualities that make the best scammers, drawing from my experiences and observations in the world of cons.

Psychological Insight

1. Empathy and Understanding:

- Emotional Intelligence: The best scammers have a keen sense of emotional intelligence. They can read people, understand their emotions, and use this knowledge to manipulate them effectively.
- Empathy: While it may seem counterintuitive, a high degree of empathy allows scammers to connect with their marks, making their lies more believable and their manipulations more effective.

2. Manipulative Skills:

- Persuasion: Masterful scammers are persuasive, able to craft convincing stories and sell them with confidence. They know how to build trust and create a sense of urgency.
- Charm and Charisma: A charismatic personality helps scammers win people over. Their charm makes others feel special and appreciated, lowering their defenses.

Intellectual Traits

1. Intelligence:

- Quick Thinking: Scammers must think on their feet, adapting to new information and changing their tactics as needed.
- Strategic Planning: Successful scams require meticulous planning and foresight. The best scammers are strategic thinkers who can anticipate potential obstacles and plan accordingly.

2. Creativity:

- Innovative Ideas: Creativity allows scammers to come up with new and unique cons, staying ahead of law enforcement and avoiding detection.
- Problem-Solving: Scammers often encounter unexpected challenges. Creative problem-solving skills enable them to navigate these hurdles effectively.

Technical Proficiency

1. Tech Savvy:

- Understanding Technology: In the modern age, many scams involve sophisticated technology. Scammers who excel in this area understand how to use technology to their advantage, from spoofing calls to creating convincing fake websites.
- Cyber Skills: Knowledge of hacking, phishing, and other cyber techniques can enhance a scammer's ability to deceive and manipulate their targets.

2. Financial Acumen:

- Knowledge of Financial Systems: A deep understanding of financial systems, including how money is transferred and laundered, helps scammers execute their cons without getting caught.
- Investment and Market Savvy: Scammers who can talk convincingly about investments and markets can pull off elaborate financial cons, like Ponzi schemes or fake investment opportunities.

Behavioral Traits

1. Confidence:

- Self-Assuredness: Confidence is key in executing a scam. The best scammers believe in their own lies, which helps them sell their stories convincingly.
- Fearlessness: Taking risks is part of the job. Successful scammers are fearless, willing to push boundaries and take bold actions to achieve their goals.

2. Adaptability:

- Flexibility: The ability to adapt to changing situations and modify plans on the fly is crucial. Scammers often need to think quickly and change their approach based on the mark's reactions.
- Resilience: Rejection and failure are part of the game. The best scammers are resilient, able to bounce back from setbacks and continue their operations with renewed vigor.

Ethical Ambiguity

1. Lack of Conscience:

- Moral Flexibility: Scammers often operate in moral gray areas. The best scammers can justify their actions and operate without being burdened by guilt or a strong sense of right and wrong.
- Desensitization: Over time, successful scammers become desensitized to the harm they cause, enabling them to continue their activities without being emotionally affected.

2. Narcissism:

- Self-Importance: A degree of narcissism can help scammers believe that they deserve what they're taking and that they are smarter than their marks and the authorities.
- Lack of Empathy: While empathy helps in understanding and manipulating marks, a lack of genuine empathy prevents scammers from feeling remorse for their actions.

Social Skills

1. Networking:

- Building Contacts: Successful scammers often operate within networks, collaborating with others who have complementary skills. Building and maintaining these networks is crucial.
- Leveraging Relationships: Scammers can leverage existing relationships and social connections to find new marks and execute their cons more effectively.

2. Observational Skills:

- Attention to Detail: Observing and understanding small details about their marks can provide valuable insights that make scams more convincing.
- Situational Awareness: Being aware of their surroundings and the context in which they are operating helps scammers avoid detection and stay one step ahead.

Conclusion

The best scammers are a unique blend of intellect, charisma, and moral ambiguity. They possess a deep understanding of human psychology, are quick thinkers and adaptors, and have the technical and financial knowledge to pull off complex cons. Their confidence and fearlessness drive them to take bold actions, while their lack of conscience and narcissistic traits allow them to operate without remorse.

While these traits and skills can lead to significant success in the world of scams, they come with a heavy ethical burden. The impact on victims is severe, causing financial loss and emotional trauma. Understanding the anatomy of a scammer provides insight into how these individuals operate and highlights the importance of vigilance and skepticism in protecting oneself from their manipulations.

Chapter 12: The Scammers' Club

In the hidden corners of the world, there exists a society of elite scammers who have risen to the pinnacle of their deceptive craft. These individuals have amassed fortunes through their illicit activities, and they come together in an exclusive group known as the Scammers' Club. This secretive organization owns a private island where they throw lavish parties, celebrating their ill-gotten gains and sharing stories of their exploits. This chapter delves into the inner workings of this clandestine group and the extravagant lifestyle they lead on their secluded paradise.

The Origins of the Scammers' Club

The Scammers' Club was founded by a group of highly successful con artists who recognized the value of networking and collaboration. These individuals, each a master in their own right, came together to create a support system where they could share techniques, resources, and protection from law enforcement.

1. Founding Members:

- The Mastermind: The leader of the group, known only as "The Mastermind," is a former investment banker who turned to scamming after a high-profile fraud case. His knowledge of finance and strategic thinking made him the natural choice to lead the club.

- The Charmer: A charismatic and persuasive individual, The Charmer is known for his ability to manipulate people effortlessly. His charm and social skills make him invaluable in recruiting new members.
- The Tech Whiz: An expert in hacking and cybercrime, The Tech Whiz provides the group with cutting-edge technology and security measures, ensuring their activities remain undetected.

2. Membership:

- Membership is by invitation only, with existing members vouching for potential new recruits. This ensures that only the most skilled and trustworthy scammers are allowed into the fold.
- The club boasts a diverse membership, including hackers, identity thieves, con artists, and financial fraudsters from around the world.

The Private Island

The Scammers' Club's private island, known as "Paradise Cove," is a tropical haven located in an undisclosed location. This island serves as both a sanctuary and a playground for the club's members, providing them with a safe space to relax and revel in their successes.

1. Acquisition and Secrecy:

- The island was acquired through a series of complex transactions designed to obscure the true ownership. Shell companies and offshore accounts were used to ensure that the purchase could not be traced back to the Scammers' Club.
- Access to the island is strictly controlled, with members arriving by private jet or yacht. The island is equipped with state-of-the-art security measures, including surveillance systems and armed guards.

2. Luxurious Amenities:

- Mansions and Villas: The island features opulent mansions and private villas, each designed to cater to the tastes of its occupants. Lavish interiors, private pools, and breathtaking views are standard.
- Entertainment Facilities: Paradise Cove boasts world-class entertainment facilities, including a private beach, golf course, spa, and a casino. Members can indulge in their favorite pastimes without fear of exposure.
- Technology Hub: The island houses a high-tech command center, where The Tech Whiz and his team monitor global activities, hack into systems, and provide cybersecurity for the members.

The Extravagant Parties

The Scammers' Club is renowned for its extravagant parties, which are the highlight of life on Paradise

Cove. These events are legendary for their opulence, excess, and exclusivity, attracting the crème de la crème of the criminal underworld.

1. Invitations and Themes:

- Invitations to the parties are coveted and only extended to members and select guests who have proven their worth. The themes of the parties vary, ranging from masquerade balls to tropical luaus, each meticulously planned and executed.
- Themes often reflect the latest trends or commemorate significant heists and cons pulled off by members.

2. Decadent Activities:

- Gourmet Feasts: World-renowned chefs are flown in to prepare gourmet meals, featuring the finest ingredients and exotic dishes. Lavish banquets are held on the beach, in the mansions, or aboard luxury yachts.
- Live Entertainment: The parties feature live entertainment, including performances by famous musicians, circus acts, and private theater productions. Fireworks displays light up the night sky, adding to the spectacle.
- Games and Competitions: Members partake in high-stakes games and competitions, from poker tournaments to treasure hunts across the island. Prizes often include rare artifacts, luxury goods, and even cryptocurrency.

3. Networking and Collaboration:

- These gatherings provide an opportunity for members to network, share stories, and collaborate on future cons. The parties serve as a platform for exchanging ideas, forming alliances, and planning new schemes.
- The Mastermind often uses these events to announce major plans and initiatives, rallying the members for large-scale operations.

The Dark Side of Paradise

While the Scammers' Club may appear to be a paradise for its members, it is not without its darker aspects. The luxurious lifestyle and sense of invincibility can breed arrogance, rivalry, and paranoia.

1. Internal Conflicts:

- Power Struggles: Despite the camaraderie, power struggles and rivalries are common. Members vie for influence and status within the group, leading to tension and occasional confrontations.
- Betrayals: Trust is a fragile commodity among scammers. Betrayals and double-crosses are not uncommon, as members seek to outmaneuver one another for personal gain.

2. Law Enforcement Pressure:

- Increased Scrutiny: As the activities of the Scammers' Club attract more attention, law enforcement agencies around the world have intensified their efforts to infiltrate and dismantle the organization.

- **Undercover Operations:** Undercover agents have attempted to penetrate the club, posing as potential members or associates. The Tech Whiz's security measures are constantly tested by these efforts.

Conclusion

The Scammers' Club represents the pinnacle of the criminal underworld, a hidden society where the world's most successful con artists come together to celebrate their wealth and ingenuity. Paradise Cove is both a sanctuary and a stage for their excesses, a place where they can indulge in their desires and plot their next moves.

Yet, beneath the surface of this idyllic existence lies a world of intrigue, power struggles, and constant danger. The very traits that make these individuals successful scammers—intelligence, adaptability, and a lack of conscience—also ensure that their paradise is never truly peaceful.

As law enforcement closes in and internal tensions rise, the future of the Scammers' Club hangs in the balance. The private island may remain a symbol of their success, but it also serves as a reminder that even the most sophisticated cons eventually face the relentless pursuit of justice.

Chapter 13: Scammers in Love

Love is a complex emotion, capable of bringing out the best and the worst in people. In the shadowy world of scammers, love takes on a unique and often dangerous form. For scammers, love can be both a source of strength and a vulnerability that exposes them to risks. This chapter delves into the intricate dynamics of relationships among scammers, exploring how love influences their lives and their scams.

The Dangerous Allure

Scammers are, by nature, masters of manipulation. They understand human emotions and exploit them for personal gain. However, when scammers fall in love with each other, the lines between deception and genuine emotion blur.

1. The Initial Attraction:

- Shared Skills: Scammers are often attracted to each other because of their shared skills and understanding of the con game. They admire each other's talents and find common ground in their unconventional lifestyles.

- **Thrill of the Game:** The adrenaline rush from executing a successful scam can be addictive. When scammers share this thrill, it creates a strong bond, akin to partners in crime.

2. **Mutual Understanding:**

- **No Need for Pretenses:** In a relationship between scammers, there's no need to hide their true selves. They understand each other's motivations and the necessity of deception in their lives.
- **Shared Secrets:** The secrecy that surrounds their scams becomes a shared experience, creating a deep sense of intimacy and trust. They become each other's confidants, knowing that the other won't judge or betray them.

Case Studies of Scammer Couples

Case Study 1: Derek and Cassie

Derek, the charismatic leader of the crew, and Cassie, the tech whiz, found love amidst their shared cons. Their relationship began as a professional partnership but quickly evolved into something deeper.

1. **The Professional Bond:**

- **Complementary Skills:** Derek's charm and Cassie's technical prowess made them a formidable team. They collaborated on numerous scams, from identity theft to elaborate phishing schemes.

- Respect and Admiration: Each admired the other's expertise. Derek respected Cassie's intelligence and creativity, while Cassie was drawn to Derek's confidence and leadership.

2. The Blossoming Romance:

- Shared Thrills: The excitement of their scams brought them closer. Late-night planning sessions and the adrenaline rush from successful cons fostered a deep connection.
- Personal Confidants: They confided in each other about their pasts and dreams, creating a bond that extended beyond their professional lives.

3. Challenges and Risks:

- Jealousy and Paranoia: Despite their bond, jealousy and paranoia occasionally surfaced. Both were aware of the deceptive nature of their world, and trust was fragile.
- Increased Risk: Their relationship made them vulnerable. If one got caught, the other could be implicated. This constant fear added stress to their lives.

Case Study 2: Sara and Lenny

Sara, the master of disguise, and Lenny, the muscle of the crew, had a relationship built on mutual dependence and understanding. Their love was a mix of passion and practicality.

1. The Practical Partnership:

- Dependence: Sara relied on Lenny's strength and loyalty, while Lenny depended on Sara's cunning and adaptability. They were each other's safety nets.
- Unspoken Trust: Their relationship was based on unspoken trust. They knew they could count on each other, both in their scams and personal lives.

2. The Emotional Connection:

- Shared Vulnerabilities: Both had difficult pasts that led them to the world of scams. Sharing their vulnerabilities created a strong emotional bond.
- Support System: They supported each other through the highs and lows of their criminal careers, providing emotional stability in a chaotic world.

3. The Cost of Love:

- Risk of Exposure: Their relationship made them more conspicuous. They had to be extra cautious to avoid drawing attention to themselves.
- Emotional Toll: The constant danger took an emotional toll. The fear of losing each other or being caught was ever-present, adding strain to their relationship.

Love as a Double-Edged Sword

In the world of scammers, love is both a source of strength and a potential Achilles' heel. The following factors highlight the dual nature of love among scammers:

1. Strength and Motivation:

- Emotional Support: Love provides emotional support, helping scammers cope with the stress and dangers of their lifestyle. It offers a sense of normalcy in an otherwise deceptive world.
- Increased Motivation: Scammers in love are often more motivated to succeed. They want to protect their partner and build a future together, even if it's based on ill-gotten gains.

2. Vulnerability and Risk:

- Increased Vulnerability: Love makes scammers more vulnerable. They have someone to lose, which can lead to mistakes and increased risk-taking.
- Leverage for Enemies: Enemies or law enforcement can exploit their relationship. Threatening a loved one can force a scammer to make hasty decisions or turn against their partner.

Conclusion

Love among scammers is a complex and multifaceted phenomenon. It brings together individuals who understand and accept each other's unconventional lives, creating deep bonds based on shared experiences and mutual support. However, this love also introduces vulnerabilities and risks, making their already precarious lives even more complicated.

For scammers, love is a double-edged sword. It provides strength and motivation but also exposes them to dangers they might otherwise avoid. Navigating the treacherous waters of romance in a world built on deception requires a delicate balance of trust, caution, and unwavering loyalty. In the end, love among scammers is as thrilling and perilous as the cons they execute, a testament to the human capacity for connection even in the darkest corners of society.

Chapter 14: Handling Snitches in the Scammer's World

In the shadowy world of scams and cons, the greatest threat often comes from within. A single snitch can bring down an entire operation, leading to arrests, loss of profits, and the exposure of carefully guarded secrets. Eliminating snitches—ensuring they can't betray you—is crucial for the survival of any scammer. This chapter delves into the strategies and tactics used to handle and eliminate snitches, focusing on prevention, detection, and resolution.

Prevention: Building a Trustworthy Network

1. Recruitment and Vetting:

- Careful Selection: Recruit only those who have proven themselves trustworthy. This involves thorough background checks, often through personal connections or references within the criminal world.
- Testing Loyalty: Before bringing someone into the inner circle, test their loyalty with smaller, less critical tasks. This helps gauge their reliability and commitment.

2. Creating a Code of Silence:

- Establishing Rules: Implement a strict code of silence among members. Make it clear that any form of betrayal will not be tolerated and will have severe consequences.
- Regular Reinforcement: Regularly remind members of the importance of loyalty and the dire consequences of snitching. This can be done through meetings, communications, and by setting examples.

3. Compartmentalization:

- Need-to-Know Basis: Share information only on a need-to-know basis. This limits the amount of knowledge any one person has, reducing the risk of significant leaks if they turn.
- Segregation of Tasks: Divide tasks among members so that no one person has a complete picture of the operation. This makes it harder for any individual to provide comprehensive information if they decide to snitch.

Detection: Identifying Potential Snitches

1. Monitoring Behavior:

- Unusual Behavior: Be alert to changes in behavior. Someone who becomes overly cautious, secretive, or starts asking too many questions might be a potential snitch.
- Financial Changes: Keep an eye on sudden changes in financial status. A member who suddenly has more money or seems financially stable without clear reason might be receiving payments for information.

2. Regular Loyalty Tests:

- Controlled Information Leaks: Occasionally, provide false information to specific individuals and monitor for leaks. If the false information reaches authorities, you'll know who the snitch is.
- Surveillance: Use surveillance tactics to monitor communications and activities. This can include electronic surveillance, physical tailing, and using informants within your own organization.

3. Interrogation and Intimidation:

- Direct Confrontation: If you suspect someone, confront them directly in a controlled environment. Watch their reactions carefully; guilty individuals often exhibit telltale signs of stress and fear.
- Intimidation Tactics: Sometimes, a show of force or intimidation can elicit the truth. This can involve physical intimidation or psychological tactics like isolation and threats.

Resolution: Dealing with Confirmed Snitches

1. Neutralization:

- Isolation: Once a snitch is identified, isolate them from the rest of the group immediately to prevent further damage.
- Damage Control: Assess the extent of the information they have leaked and take steps to mitigate the damage. This may involve changing plans, moving operations, or cutting off certain activities.

2. Retribution:

- Exile: In some cases, simply exiling the snitch from the organization and ensuring they can't communicate further with authorities might be enough.
- Public Example: Making a public example of a snitch can serve as a powerful deterrent to others. This can involve a public declaration of their betrayal and the consequences they face.
- Elimination: In extreme cases, eliminating the snitch might be necessary. This is a last resort and carries significant risks, including legal consequences and potential retaliation.

3. Psychological Tactics:

- Discrediting: Discredit the snitch's information by spreading false information and creating doubt about their credibility. This can involve planting false evidence or using counterintelligence tactics.
- Fear and Intimidation: Spread rumors about the severe consequences faced by past snitches. This creates a climate of fear that discourages others from considering betrayal.

Case Study: Handling a High-Risk Snitch

Target: A member of the crew suspected of leaking information to authorities.

Execution:

1. **Behavioral Monitoring: A key member of the crew, John, started showing signs of unusual behavior. He was more secretive, avoided certain conversations, and seemed unusually nervous during meetings.**
2. **Controlled Leak: A piece of false information about an upcoming heist was shared with John. Within days, the authorities had increased surveillance in the area related to the false information.**
3. **Interrogation: John was confronted in a controlled environment. Under psychological pressure and intimidation, he eventually admitted to leaking information in exchange for a reduced sentence for a previous crime.**
4. **Neutralization: John was immediately isolated, and the crew took steps to mitigate the damage, including changing plans and moving their base of operations.**
5. **Retribution: John was made an example of. His betrayal was publicly declared within the criminal community, and he was exiled from the group. Rumors about his fate spread, reinforcing the consequences of betrayal.**

Conclusion

In the world of scams and cons, the threat of snitches is ever-present. Handling them requires a combination of prevention, detection, and decisive action. Building a trustworthy network, regularly testing loyalty, and taking swift action against confirmed snitches are crucial steps in maintaining the integrity and safety of any criminal operation.

While the strategies outlined in this chapter are effective, they also highlight the dark and dangerous nature of the scammer's world. The constant threat of betrayal and the need for ruthless measures create an environment of fear and mistrust. For scammers, eliminating snitches is not just about survival; it's about maintaining control and authority in a world where deception is the currency and trust is a rare commodity.

Chapter 15: Who is Most Likely to Get Scammed?

Scammers are adept at identifying and exploiting vulnerabilities in their targets. While anyone can fall victim to a scam, certain demographics and personality traits make some individuals more susceptible than others. In this chapter, we explore who is most likely to get scammed, examining the characteristics and circumstances that put them at greater risk.

Demographic Vulnerabilities

1. Elderly Individuals:

- Lack of Tech Savvy: Many older adults are not as familiar with modern technology, making them easy targets for online scams, phishing, and tech support fraud.
- Loneliness and Isolation: Scammers exploit the loneliness of elderly individuals by posing as friends, romantic partners, or caring professionals, gaining their trust and then exploiting them financially.
- Trusting Nature: Having grown up in a time when trust in people and institutions was higher, older adults may be less suspicious of unsolicited offers or requests.

2. Young Adults and Teens:

- Inexperience: Younger individuals, particularly teens, may lack the experience and knowledge to recognize scams. Their eagerness to engage with new opportunities can make them easy targets.
- Online Presence: With a significant portion of their lives spent online, young adults are vulnerable to social media scams, phishing, and cyberbullying.
- Desire for Quick Success: The appeal of making quick money or gaining social media fame can

lead young people to fall for investment scams, influencer scams, and get-rich-quick schemes.

3. Middle-Aged Professionals:

- Financial Responsibility: Middle-aged individuals often have substantial financial responsibilities, including mortgages, car loans, and educational expenses. Scammers exploit their need for financial stability and growth.
- Busy Lifestyles: Juggling work, family, and other responsibilities leaves little time for thorough research, making this group susceptible to investment scams, business email compromise, and identity theft.
- Online Transactions: Frequent use of online banking, shopping, and social networks increases exposure to phishing, data breaches, and online fraud.

Psychological Traits

1. Trusting and Empathetic Individuals:

- High Empathy: People who are naturally empathetic and caring are more likely to believe stories of hardship and urgent need, making them targets for charity scams, romance scams, and sob story cons.
- Trusting Nature: Individuals who tend to trust others and take things at face value are more likely to fall for scams that rely on building a quick rapport and trust.

2. Optimistic and Ambitious People:

- **Desire for Success:** Those with high aspirations and a strong desire for success may be more vulnerable to investment scams, Ponzi schemes, and multi-level marketing (MLM) scams that promise high returns and quick profits.
- **Risk-Takers:** Individuals willing to take risks for the possibility of high rewards are more likely to be drawn into gambling scams, online betting frauds, and speculative investments.

3. Individuals Facing Financial Hardship:

- Desperation: People experiencing financial difficulties are more likely to fall for scams promising debt relief, quick loans, or easy money. Their desperation can cloud their judgment and make them overlook red flags.
- Unemployment: Those out of work may be targeted by job offer scams, work-from-home schemes, and fraudulent recruitment agencies that prey on their need for income.

Circumstantial Vulnerabilities

1. Major Life Changes:

- Recent Divorce or Bereavement: Emotional distress from significant life changes, such as divorce or the death of a loved one, can make individuals more susceptible to scams. They may be seeking companionship, financial stability, or emotional support, which scammers can exploit.

- Moving or Relocation: The stress and distraction of moving to a new place can make individuals more vulnerable to moving scams, rental fraud, and utility scams.

2. Lack of Awareness and Education:

- Unawareness of Scams: People who are not aware of the various types of scams and how they operate are more likely to fall victim. Education and awareness are crucial in preventing scams.
- Low Digital Literacy: Those who are not well-versed in using digital platforms and understanding online security measures are at higher risk of online fraud, phishing, and cybercrime.

3. Overconfidence:

- Belief in One's Invulnerability: Some individuals believe they are too smart to be scammed, which can make them overconfident and less vigilant. This overconfidence can be exploited by sophisticated scammers who use psychological manipulation.

Case Studies: Real-Life Examples

Case Study 1: The Lonely Widow

- Profile: A recently widowed elderly woman, living alone and not tech-savvy.
- Scam: She was targeted by a romance scammer who posed as a kind-hearted retiree. After

months of building trust, the scammer claimed to need money for an emergency and persuaded her to send significant sums.
- Outcome: By the time she realized it was a scam, she had lost her life savings and was emotionally devastated.

Case Study 2: The Ambitious Young Professional

- Profile: A young, ambitious professional eager to invest and grow his wealth quickly.
- Scam: He was drawn into a Ponzi scheme promising high returns on cryptocurrency investments. The scheme was elaborate, with fake websites, testimonials, and even small initial returns to build trust.
- Outcome: He invested heavily and encouraged friends and family to do the same. When the scheme collapsed, he lost his investment and damaged personal relationships.

Case Study 3: The Overconfident Tech Enthusiast

- Profile: A middle-aged tech enthusiast who believed he was too savvy to be scammed.
- Scam: He fell for a sophisticated phishing email that mimicked his bank's communications perfectly. He entered his login details, which were then used to drain his accounts.
- Outcome: His overconfidence blinded him to the subtle signs of phishing, leading to significant financial loss.

Conclusion

Understanding who is most likely to get scammed helps in developing targeted prevention and education strategies. While anyone can fall victim to a scam, certain demographics, psychological traits, and circumstances increase susceptibility. By recognizing these vulnerabilities, individuals can take proactive steps to protect themselves and reduce the risk of falling prey to scammers.

Scammers exploit trust, empathy, ambition, and desperation, weaving intricate traps that appeal to their victims' hopes and fears. Awareness, education, and vigilance are crucial in defending against these threats, ensuring that fewer people fall victim to the deceptive schemes lurking in the shadows.

Chapter 16: Anyone Can Be Scammed

While it is true that certain demographics and personality traits can make individuals more susceptible to scams, the harsh reality is that anyone can be scammed. Scammers are constantly evolving their tactics, becoming more sophisticated, and exploiting even the smallest vulnerabilities. In this chapter, we will explore how no one is immune to scams, highlighting real-life examples of unexpected victims and offering strategies to mitigate the risk for everyone.

The Universal Vulnerability

1. Human Nature:

- Trust: Trust is a fundamental aspect of human relationships. Scammers exploit this basic human trait by posing as trustworthy individuals or institutions.
- Emotion: Emotions such as fear, greed, love, and desperation can cloud judgment, making even the most rational individuals susceptible to scams.
- Cognitive Biases: Cognitive biases like the optimism bias (believing that bad things happen to others, not to oneself) can lead people to underestimate the risk of being scammed.

2. Sophistication of Scams:

- Advanced Technology: Scammers use advanced technology to create highly convincing fake websites, emails, and phone calls. Deepfake technology, for example, can create realistic videos of people saying things they never actually said.
- Social Engineering: Scammers are skilled at social engineering, manipulating people into divulging confidential information or performing actions they wouldn't normally do.
- Personalization: With access to vast amounts of personal data, scammers can personalize their

approaches, making their scams even more convincing.

Real-Life Examples of Unexpected Victims

1. The CEO Phishing Scam:

- Profile: A successful CEO of a large corporation, known for his tech-savvy and cautious nature.
- Scam: The CEO received an email that appeared to be from a trusted vendor, complete with accurate details about an ongoing business deal. The email requested urgent payment to avoid disrupting the project.
- Outcome: The CEO authorized a wire transfer of millions of dollars before realizing the email was a sophisticated phishing attempt. The funds were quickly moved through multiple accounts, making recovery difficult.

2. The Financial Expert Ponzi Scheme:

- Profile: A renowned financial expert with decades of experience in investment management.
- Scam: The expert was approached by a charismatic individual offering an exclusive investment opportunity with guaranteed high returns. The scheme was well-researched, using industry jargon and impressive fake performance records.
- Outcome: Convinced by the elaborate setup, the financial expert invested heavily and encouraged clients to do the same. When the Ponzi scheme collapsed, the losses were

catastrophic, damaging reputations and finances.

3. The Tech-Savvy Teen Hacker Trap:

- Profile: A tech-savvy teenager known for his programming skills and online security awareness.
- Scam: The teen was lured into a hacking community offering tools and resources. After participating in discussions and sharing some personal exploits, he was tricked into downloading a tool that was actually malware.
- Outcome: The malware compromised his system, stealing personal information and financial data. Despite his expertise, the teen found himself a victim of a targeted scam.

Strategies to Mitigate Risk

1. Education and Awareness:

- Continuous Learning: Stay informed about the latest scams and tactics. Scammers are constantly evolving, so ongoing education is crucial.
- Training Programs: Participate in or provide regular training programs on recognizing and avoiding scams. This is particularly important in professional settings.

2. Skepticism and Verification:

- Healthy Skepticism: Cultivate a healthy level of skepticism, especially when dealing with unsolicited communications or offers that seem too good to be true.

- Verification Processes: Always verify the authenticity of requests for personal information or financial transactions. Use trusted contact methods to confirm legitimacy.

3. Security Measures:

- Strong Passwords: Use strong, unique passwords for different accounts and enable two-factor authentication wherever possible.
- Updated Systems: Keep your software and systems updated to protect against vulnerabilities and malware.
- Data Privacy: Be mindful of the personal information you share online. Limit the amount of data available on public platforms and adjust privacy settings accordingly.

4. Emotional Control:

- Pause and Reflect: Take a moment to pause and reflect before acting on emotional triggers. Scammers often create a sense of urgency to cloud judgment.
- Seek Advice: Consult with trusted friends, family, or professionals before making significant decisions or transactions, especially when under emotional stress.

5. Reporting and Support:

- Report Scams: Report scams to relevant authorities and platforms to help prevent others from falling victim.
- Seek Support: If you have been scammed, seek support from legal, financial, and emotional resources to manage the aftermath effectively.

Conclusion

Scammers are highly skilled at exploiting human vulnerabilities, and their tactics are becoming increasingly sophisticated. No one is immune to scams, regardless of their age, profession, or level of awareness. Recognizing this universal vulnerability is the first step in protecting oneself and others.

By staying informed, practicing skepticism, implementing robust security measures, and managing emotions, individuals can reduce their risk of falling victim to scams. Additionally, fostering a culture of reporting and support helps create a collective defense against the ever-evolving threat of scams.

In the end, awareness and vigilance are our best tools in the fight against scammers. By understanding that anyone can be scammed, we can take proactive steps to safeguard ourselves and build a more resilient society.

Chapter 17: Scammers on the Dark Web

The dark web is a hidden part of the internet that is only accessible through special software, such as Tor, designed to ensure anonymity and privacy. While it is used for legitimate purposes, such as maintaining privacy in oppressive regimes, it is also a haven for illicit activities, including scams. This chapter delves into the shadowy world of dark web scammers, exploring their methods, the types of scams they run, and the risks they pose.

The Dark Web Ecosystem

1. Anonymity and Encryption:

- Anonymity: The dark web's architecture ensures that users' identities and locations remain hidden. This anonymity is a double-edged sword, protecting privacy while also facilitating criminal activities.
- Encryption: Communications on the dark web are heavily encrypted, making it difficult for law enforcement to track and intercept messages.

2. Marketplaces and Forums:

- Marketplaces: Dark web marketplaces operate similarly to e-commerce sites, offering a range of illegal goods and services, including drugs, weapons, stolen data, and counterfeit documents.
- Forums: Discussion forums on the dark web allow scammers to share tips, trade resources, and collaborate on schemes. These forums are often invitation-only, fostering a sense of community among cybercriminals.

Common Dark Web Scams

1. Phishing Kits and Services:

- Phishing Kits: Scammers on the dark web sell phishing kits—pre-packaged tools that make it easy to launch phishing attacks. These kits often include templates for fake websites, email scripts, and automated tools.
- Phishing Services: For those lacking the technical skills, some dark web vendors offer phishing as a service, conducting attacks on behalf of clients for a fee.

2. Ransomware and Malware:

- Ransomware Kits: Ransomware kits allow scammers to deploy malware that encrypts victims' files, demanding payment for decryption. These kits often come with customer support and updates.
- Malware Marketplaces: Dark web marketplaces offer a range of malware, from keyloggers to spyware, which scammers use to steal sensitive information.

3. Identity Theft and Fraud:

- Stolen Data: The dark web is a marketplace for stolen personal data, including credit card numbers, social security numbers, and login credentials. Scammers buy this data to commit identity theft and fraud.
- Counterfeit Documents: Scammers also sell counterfeit documents, such as passports, driver's licenses, and ID cards, which can be used to create false identities.

4. Investment Scams and Ponzi Schemes:

- **Cryptocurrency Scams:** Cryptocurrency scams are rampant on the dark web. Scammers promise high returns on investments in new cryptocurrencies or mining operations, only to disappear with the funds.
- **Ponzi Schemes:** Ponzi schemes on the dark web attract victims with promises of quick profits from investments in illegal activities or new technologies. Early investors are paid with funds from newer investors, until the scheme collapses.

5. Social Engineering Services:

- **Custom Scams:** Some dark web scammers offer custom social engineering services, designing bespoke scams tailored to specific targets. These services can include detailed research on the target and personalized attack strategies.
- **Social Media Exploitation:** Scammers exploit social media platforms to gather information about victims, creating convincing phishing attacks or impersonating friends and family members.

The Risks and Consequences

1. Legal and Financial Risks:

- **Prosecution:** Engaging in scams on the dark web carries significant legal risks. Law enforcement agencies around the world are increasingly focusing on dark web activities, leading to high-profile arrests and prosecutions.

- Financial Loss: Scammers face financial risks, as dark web transactions are often conducted in volatile cryptocurrencies. Additionally, disputes between criminals are unlikely to be resolved legally, leading to potential losses.

2. Ethical and Moral Implications:

- Exploitation of Vulnerability: Dark web scams exploit the most vulnerable, causing significant financial and emotional harm to victims.
- Moral Decay: Participation in dark web scams can lead to a further erosion of ethical boundaries, fostering a culture of deception and criminality.

Real-Life Examples of Dark Web Scams

Example 1: The Silk Road:

- Background: The Silk Road was one of the most infamous dark web marketplaces, known for selling illegal drugs, weapons, and other illicit goods.
- Scams: While the Silk Road provided a platform for various illegal activities, it was also a hotbed for scams. Vendors would often take payment without delivering goods, or sell counterfeit products.
- Outcome: The Silk Road was eventually shut down by law enforcement, and its founder, Ross

Ulbricht, was arrested and sentenced to life in prison.

Example 2: AlphaBay:

- Background: AlphaBay was another major dark web marketplace, offering a wide range of illegal goods and services.
- Scams: AlphaBay was notorious for hosting scams, including phishing services, ransomware kits, and counterfeit documents. Many buyers were defrauded by vendors who disappeared after receiving payment.
- Outcome: AlphaBay was shut down in a coordinated international law enforcement operation, leading to several arrests and significant disruption of dark web activities.

Protecting Yourself from Dark Web Scams

1. Awareness and Education:

- Stay Informed: Be aware of the types of scams that originate from the dark web and how they operate. This knowledge can help you recognize and avoid potential threats.
- Cybersecurity Training: Regularly participate in cybersecurity training to learn how to protect yourself from phishing, malware, and other online threats.

2. Strong Security Measures:

- Use Strong Passwords: Use strong, unique passwords for all your accounts and enable two-factor authentication wherever possible.
- Update Software: Keep your software and systems updated to protect against vulnerabilities and malware.

3. Vigilance and Skepticism:

- Verify Sources: Be skeptical of unsolicited communications and offers that seem too good to be true. Always verify the source before providing personal information or making payments.
- Monitor Accounts: Regularly monitor your financial accounts for any suspicious activity and report any unauthorized transactions immediately.

Conclusion

The dark web is a breeding ground for sophisticated scams that exploit the anonymity and encryption it offers. While the allure of the dark web can be strong, it is fraught with legal, financial, and ethical risks. Anyone can fall victim to these scams, regardless of their background or level of awareness.

Understanding the ecosystem of the dark web, the common scams that thrive there, and the risks involved is crucial for protecting oneself. By staying informed, practicing strong security measures, and maintaining vigilance, individuals can reduce their risk of falling victim to the deceptive schemes that lurk in the shadows of the dark web.

Chapter 18: Call Girl Scams

The world of call girl scams is a complex and dark facet of the broader landscape of deception. These scams exploit the human desire for intimacy and companionship, leveraging the anonymity of the internet and the allure of illicit encounters. In this chapter, we will explore the various types of call girl scams, how they operate, and the profound impact they can have on their victims.

The Mechanics of Call Girl Scams

1. Online Advertisements:

- Fake Profiles: Scammers create fake profiles on adult websites, social media platforms, and classified ads. These profiles feature attractive photos (often stolen from real individuals) and enticing descriptions.
- Targeting: These ads are designed to lure individuals seeking companionship, promising discretion and satisfaction.

2. Initial Contact:

- Communication: Interested individuals make contact through phone calls, text messages, or online chat services. Scammers maintain a professional and seductive demeanor to build trust and anticipation.
- Deposit Requests: Before meeting, the scammer often requests a deposit or advance payment to secure the booking. This is usually framed as a standard procedure to ensure the client's commitment and seriousness.

3. Payment and Escalation:

- Payment Methods: Payments are typically requested via untraceable methods such as prepaid debit cards, gift cards, cryptocurrency, or direct bank transfers. This minimizes the risk of tracking the scammer.
- Additional Fees: After the initial payment, the scammer may introduce additional fees for "unexpected" expenses, such as transportation, security, or hotel costs. Each payment is framed as necessary to proceed with the encounter.

4. The No-Show:

- Disappearance: Once the scammer has extracted as much money as possible, they disappear, ceasing all communication. The victim is left without the promised encounter and has little recourse for recovering their money.

Types of Call Girl Scams

1. Fake Escort Services:

- Professional Websites: Scammers create professional-looking websites for fake escort services. These sites often feature sophisticated design, customer testimonials, and a booking system.
- Client Screening: To build credibility, the scam may involve a client screening process, collecting personal information and references. This not only reassures the victim but also adds to the scammer's leverage.
- High Fees: Clients are charged high fees for memberships, bookings, and additional services, with no intention of delivering on any promises.

2. Blackmail and Extortion:

- Recording Interactions: Scammers may record interactions, including explicit conversations and photos exchanged during initial communications.
- Threats: Once they have compromising material, they threaten to expose the victim to their family, friends, or employer unless a significant sum of money is paid.
- Ongoing Demands: Even after an initial payment, the blackmailer may continue to demand money, creating a never-ending cycle of extortion.

3. Honeypot Scams:

- Building Trust: The scammer engages in prolonged conversations to build trust and emotional connections with the victim. They may pose as an individual looking for a genuine relationship.

- **Requests for Help: After establishing trust, the scammer invents a crisis or emergency, requesting financial help. Common scenarios include medical emergencies, travel expenses, or legal troubles.**
- **Disappearance: Once the victim provides financial assistance, the scammer disappears, often blocking all contact methods.**

4. The In-Person Robbery:

- **Arranged Meeting: The scammer arranges to meet the victim in person, typically in a private setting such as a hotel room or apartment.**
- **Ambush: Instead of the promised encounter, the victim is ambushed by accomplices, robbed, and sometimes physically assaulted.**
- **Limited Recourse: Due to the illegal nature of the meeting, victims are often reluctant to report the crime to authorities, fearing legal repercussions or public shame.**

Real-Life Case Studies

Case Study 1: The High-End Escort Scam

- **Profile: A businessman looking for discreet companionship from a high-end escort service.**
- **Scam: He found a professional-looking website and paid an initial deposit for a booking. The service then requested additional fees for security and transportation.**

- Outcome: After several payments totaling thousands of dollars, the escort never showed up, and the website disappeared. Attempts to contact the service were met with silence.

Case Study 2: The Blackmail Trap

- Profile: A married professional seeking discreet encounters.
- Scam: He communicated with an attractive call girl who requested explicit photos to ensure he was genuine. Soon after, he received threats demanding money to prevent the photos from being sent to his family and employer.
- Outcome: He paid the blackmailer multiple times, fearing exposure, but the demands continued until he sought legal advice and reported the extortion.

Case Study 3: The Honeypot Scheme

- Profile: A lonely individual seeking companionship and possibly a relationship.
- Scam: He developed an online relationship with a call girl who eventually claimed to need money for a medical emergency. He sent her several thousand dollars.
- Outcome: After receiving the money, the call girl vanished, leaving him heartbroken and financially devastated.

Preventing Call Girl Scams

1. Verification and Research:

- Verify Credentials: Use multiple sources to verify the legitimacy of any escort service or individual. Look for reviews, third-party references, and check if the photos used are genuine.
- Background Checks: Perform a reverse image search on profile photos and verify any provided personal details.

2. Avoiding Advance Payments:

- No Prepayments: Avoid making any payments before meeting in person. Legitimate services typically do not require advance payments through untraceable methods.
- Secure Payment Methods: If payment is necessary, use secure and traceable methods. Avoid gift cards, prepaid cards, or cryptocurrencies for initial transactions.

3. Protecting Personal Information:

- Minimal Disclosure: Limit the amount of personal information shared during initial communications. Avoid sharing explicit photos or sensitive details.
- Use Aliases: Consider using aliases and separate contact information to protect your identity and privacy.

4. Reporting and Seeking Help:

- Report Scams: If you fall victim to a scam, report it to the relevant authorities and platforms. Many law enforcement agencies have cybercrime units that can assist.

- Seek Legal Advice: Consult with a legal professional if you are being blackmailed or extorted. They can provide guidance on protecting your rights and stopping the extortion.

Conclusion

Call girl scams are a dark and deceptive aspect of the broader scam landscape, preying on individuals' desires for intimacy and companionship. These scams can have devastating financial and emotional consequences, exploiting vulnerabilities and leveraging fear and shame to maintain control over victims.

Understanding the mechanics of these scams, recognizing the signs, and taking proactive steps to protect oneself are crucial in preventing victimization. By staying informed and vigilant, individuals can navigate the complex world of online interactions and avoid falling prey to the deceptive tactics of call girl scammers.

Chapter 19: Watch Out for Junkies

Navigating the complex world of scams requires vigilance and awareness, especially when dealing with individuals struggling with addiction. Junkies, or individuals heavily addicted to drugs, often resort to scams and deceit to fund their habits. Their desperation and unpredictability make them particularly dangerous and challenging to handle. This chapter explores the various scams perpetrated by junkies, the risks they pose, and strategies to protect oneself from falling victim to their schemes.

The Desperation of Addiction

1. The Impact of Addiction:

- Constant Need for Funds: Addiction creates a relentless need for money to purchase drugs. This need drives addicts to engage in scams and criminal activities.
- Impaired Judgment: Drugs impair judgment and decision-making abilities, leading addicts to take greater risks and act impulsively.
- Moral Compromise: The desperation to satisfy their addiction often leads addicts to compromise their morals and engage in deceitful behavior.

Common Scams by Junkies

1. Sob Stories and Panhandling:

- Heart-Wrenching Tales: Junkies often concoct sob stories to elicit sympathy and money from strangers. These tales typically involve fabricated emergencies, such as needing money for a bus ticket, medical treatment, or to support a family.
- Aggressive Panhandling: They may approach individuals in public places, aggressively asking for money under the guise of immediate need.

2. Petty Theft and Resale:

- Stealing for Quick Cash: Junkies frequently engage in petty theft, stealing items from homes, cars, and stores. They often target easily accessible and resellable items like electronics, jewelry, and personal belongings.
- Pawnshops and Street Markets: Stolen items are quickly resold to pawnshops or on the streets at a fraction of their value to generate quick cash.

3. Fake Fundraising:

- Bogus Charities: Junkies may pose as representatives of non-existent charities, collecting donations for fabricated causes. They might use fake identification and printed materials to appear legitimate.
- Door-to-Door Scams: Going door-to-door, they solicit donations for fake causes, preying on the goodwill of residents.

4. Identity Theft and Fraud:

- Stealing Personal Information: Addicts may resort to identity theft, stealing personal information from mail, trash, or hacked accounts. This information is used to open fraudulent accounts, make purchases, or secure loans.
- Check Fraud: They may steal checkbooks and forge signatures to write checks for cash or goods.

5. Drug Trade and Scams:

- **Selling Fake Drugs: Desperate for money, junkies may sell counterfeit drugs, passing off household items or harmless substances as narcotics.**
- **Shortchanging: In drug transactions, they may shortchange buyers, providing less product than promised or cutting it with harmful substances.**

Real-Life Case Studies

Case Study 1: The Sympathy Seeker

- **Profile: A young woman struggling with addiction, frequently seen panhandling near busy intersections.**
- **Scam: She approaches passersby with a tearful story about needing money to visit her sick child in the hospital. Her appearance and emotional plea elicit sympathy and small donations from many.**
- **Outcome: Despite collecting significant amounts of money daily, she uses all of it to fund her addiction, perpetuating her cycle of deceit and dependency.**

Case Study 2: The Petty Thief

- **Profile: A middle-aged man with a long history of drug addiction and petty crime.**
- **Scam: He targets suburban neighborhoods, breaking into cars and stealing valuable items like GPS devices, wallets, and electronics. He quickly sells these items to pawnshops.**

- Outcome: The stolen items generate enough money to sustain his addiction, but his repeated offenses eventually lead to his arrest and incarceration.

Case Study 3: The Fake Charity Worker

- Profile: A woman in her thirties, using her appearance and demeanor to pose as a legitimate charity worker.
- Scam: She goes door-to-door in affluent neighborhoods, claiming to collect donations for a children's cancer charity. She carries fake brochures and a donation box to appear authentic.
- Outcome: Residents, moved by her story, make generous donations. The money is immediately used to buy drugs, and she moves to a different neighborhood before suspicion arises.

Protecting Yourself from Junkie Scams

1. Awareness and Vigilance:

- Be Skeptical: Approach unsolicited requests for money or donations with caution. Verify the legitimacy of any charity or cause before donating.
- Secure Personal Information: Shred sensitive documents before discarding them and monitor your mail to prevent theft of personal information.

2. Protecting Property:

- **Lock Doors and Windows:** Ensure your home and vehicles are always locked, even when you are present. Install security systems and cameras to deter theft.
- **Avoid Displaying Valuables:** Do not leave valuable items in plain sight within your home or car. Keep them out of sight or securely locked away.

3. Financial Security:

- **Monitor Accounts:** Regularly check your bank and credit card statements for unauthorized transactions. Report any suspicious activity immediately.
- **Use Strong Passwords:** Protect your online accounts with strong, unique passwords and enable two-factor authentication where possible.

4. Reporting and Support:

- **Report Scams:** If you encounter a suspected scam, report it to local authorities or relevant organizations. This can help prevent others from falling victim.
- **Seek Help for Addicts:** If you know someone struggling with addiction, encourage them to seek professional help and support. Addressing the root cause of their behavior can reduce their reliance on scams.

Conclusion

Dealing with scammers who are driven by addiction requires a combination of awareness, vigilance, and empathy. While it is essential to protect oneself from their deceitful tactics, it is also important to recognize the underlying struggles that drive their behavior. By understanding the mechanics of junkie scams and taking proactive measures to safeguard against them, individuals can reduce their risk of falling victim to these desperate and often dangerous schemes. Additionally, supporting efforts to address addiction and provide rehabilitation can help mitigate the root causes of these scams, ultimately benefiting both the individuals involved and the broader community.

Chapter 20: The Rise and Fall of a Professional Female Scammer

The Glittering Rise

1. Early Beginnings:

- Charm and Wit: Linda Morgan was born with an innate charm and sharp wit. From a young age, she realized that she had a talent for persuasion and manipulation.
- First Scams: Her early scams were small-time cons, swindling classmates and neighbors. She

quickly learned the art of deception and honed her skills.

2. Ascending the Ranks:

- High Society Scams: As she grew older, Linda set her sights higher. She infiltrated high society, using her beauty and charisma to gain access to exclusive circles. She would attend galas, fundraisers, and charity events, charming wealthy businessmen and socialites.
- Corporate Fraud: Linda developed intricate schemes to defraud corporations. She posed as a high-level consultant, forging documents and using insider information to embezzle millions. Her victims were left bankrupt and bewildered, never suspecting the elegant woman who had dined at their tables.

3. Building a Network:

- Accomplices: Linda built a network of accomplices, including hackers, forgers, and even corrupt officials. This network enabled her to pull off increasingly complex and lucrative scams.
- Luxury Lifestyle: With her ill-gotten gains, Linda led a life of luxury. She lived in a penthouse, drove expensive cars, and vacationed in exotic locales. Her children, each from different relationships, were cared for by nannies and attended private schools.

The Downward Spiral

1. Addiction Takes Hold:

- Experimentation: At the height of her success, Linda began experimenting with drugs. Initially, it was just recreational use at parties. However, she soon became addicted to methamphetamine.
- Escalation: Her addiction escalated rapidly. She began using meth daily, neglecting her schemes and her children. Her behavior became erratic, and she started making mistakes.

2. Financial Collapse:

- Neglecting the Network: Linda's addiction caused her to neglect her network of accomplices. Without her careful coordination, the scams began to fall apart. Accomplices were arrested, and investigations closed in on her operations.
- Squandering Wealth: The wealth she had amassed was quickly squandered on drugs, parties, and fleeting pleasures. Bills piled up, and debts mounted. Her luxurious lifestyle crumbled around her.

3. Personal Turmoil:

- Strained Relationships: Her relationships with the fathers of her children deteriorated. They distanced themselves, taking legal action to gain custody of their children. Linda was left isolated and without support.
- Neglecting Her Children: Her children, once cared for in luxury, were neglected. Social services intervened, and they were placed in foster care.

The Tragic End

1. Homelessness:

- **Eviction:** Unable to pay her bills, Linda was evicted from her penthouse. She bounced from one cheap motel to another, eventually ending up on the streets.
- **Desperation:** Desperate for her next fix, she resorted to petty crimes and begging. The woman who had once conned millions now scavenged for food and shelter.

2. Living in a Dumpster:

- **Dumpster Dwelling:** Linda found a temporary refuge in a large dumpster behind a rundown building. It provided some semblance of shelter, away from the dangers of the streets.
- **Hopelessness:** Strung out and hopeless, Linda spent her days and nights in a haze, barely aware of her surroundings.

3. The Final Tragedy:

- **Passing Out:** One night, after a particularly heavy dose of meth, Linda passed out in the dumpster. She was oblivious to the world around her, lost in the depths of her addiction.
- **Tragic End:** In the early hours of the morning, a garbage truck arrived to empty the dumpster. The driver, unaware of Linda's presence, operated the compactor. Linda was caught in the machinery, her life tragically ending in a moment of crushing oblivion.

Reflection and Aftermath

Linda Morgan's story is a stark reminder of the dangers of addiction and the devastating impact it can have on even the most successful individuals. Her rise to the top of the criminal underworld was matched only by her precipitous fall, fueled by her addiction to methamphetamine.

Her children, left to navigate life without their mother, faced their own challenges in the foster care system. Linda's network of accomplices either faced legal consequences or faded into obscurity, their once-powerful syndicate dismantled.

Linda's life, marked by deception and manipulation, ultimately ended in a tragic and lonely death. Her story serves as a cautionary tale about the perils of a life built on lies and the destructive power of addiction.

Chapter 21: Protecting Yourself from Scammers and Cons

In a world where scams and cons are increasingly sophisticated, it's essential to stay vigilant and informed to protect yourself from falling victim to these schemes. This chapter provides practical strategies and tips to safeguard your finances, personal information, and well-being from scammers.

Understanding the Tactics

1. Common Scams:

- Phishing: Scammers use fake emails, texts, or websites to steal personal information.
- Impersonation Scams: Posing as trusted individuals or organizations, scammers ask for money or personal details.
- Online Shopping Scams: Fake e-commerce sites or sellers take your money without delivering the goods.
- Investment Scams: Promises of high returns on investments that are either non-existent or highly risky.

Protecting Your Personal Information

1. Secure Your Digital Footprint:

- Strong Passwords: Use complex passwords and change them regularly. Consider using a password manager.
- Two-Factor Authentication: Enable two-factor authentication (2FA) for an added layer of security on your accounts.
- Regular Updates: Keep your software and devices updated to protect against vulnerabilities.

2. Be Cautious with Personal Information:

- Limit Sharing: Avoid sharing personal information on social media or with unknown entities.
- Shred Documents: Shred sensitive documents before discarding them to prevent identity theft.
- Monitor Your Accounts: Regularly check your bank and credit card statements for unauthorized transactions.

Recognizing Red Flags

1. Too Good to Be True:

- Unrealistic Offers: Be skeptical of offers that promise large sums of money for little effort or investment.
- High-Pressure Tactics: Scammers often create a sense of urgency to push you into making quick decisions.

2. Verification is Key:

- Verify Sources: Always verify the legitimacy of the person or organization contacting you. Use official contact information from trusted sources.
- Check URLs: Look closely at URLs for online transactions. Secure websites should start with "https://" and have a padlock icon.

Financial Protection

1. Use Secure Payment Methods:

    - Credit Cards: Use credit cards for online purchases as they offer better fraud protection compared to debit cards.
    - Reputable Platforms: Only make payments through secure and reputable platforms.

2. Be Wary of Requests for Payment:

    - Untraceable Methods: Be cautious of requests for payment via gift cards, prepaid debit cards, wire transfers, or cryptocurrencies.
    - Advance Payments: Avoid making advance payments for goods or services, especially to unfamiliar vendors.

Cybersecurity Measures

1. Protect Your Devices:

    - Antivirus Software: Install and maintain reputable antivirus software on your devices.
    - Firewalls: Use firewalls to protect your home network from unauthorized access.

2. Safe Browsing Practices:

    - Avoid Public Wi-Fi: Avoid conducting sensitive transactions over public Wi-Fi networks. Use a Virtual Private Network (VPN) if necessary.

- Be Wary of Links and Attachments: Avoid clicking on links or downloading attachments from unknown sources.

Educating Yourself and Others

1. Stay Informed:

- Current Scams: Keep up-to-date with the latest scams and tactics used by scammers. Many government and consumer protection websites provide regular updates.
- Learn from Others: Share information about scams with friends and family to raise awareness and prevent them from falling victim.

2. Use Resources:

- Consumer Protection Agencies: Utilize resources from consumer protection agencies, such as the Federal Trade Commission (FTC) in the U.S., which offers advice and support for scam victims.
- Online Courses: Consider taking online courses or attending seminars on cybersecurity and fraud prevention.

Responding to Scams

1. If You Suspect a Scam:

- Do Not Engage: Do not respond to suspicious emails, texts, or calls. Disengage and verify the source independently.
- Report the Scam: Report the scam to relevant authorities, such as consumer protection agencies, financial institutions, or local law enforcement.

2. If You Fall Victim:

- Contact Financial Institutions: Immediately contact your bank or credit card company to report the fraud and take steps to protect your accounts.
- Change Passwords: Change your passwords for any accounts that may have been compromised.
- Monitor Your Credit: Consider placing a fraud alert on your credit report and monitoring your credit for any suspicious activity.

Practical Scenarios and Tips

Scenario 1: The Phishing Email

- Recognize: You receive an email claiming to be from your bank, asking you to verify your account information.
- Protect: Check the sender's email address for inconsistencies, avoid clicking on links, and contact your bank directly using a known, legitimate phone number.

Scenario 2: The Fake Charity

- Recognize: You receive a call from a charity asking for donations after a natural disaster.
- Protect: Research the charity online, check for reviews and ratings, and donate directly through the charity's official website rather than over the phone.

Scenario 3: The Investment Opportunity

- Recognize: A friend tells you about a new investment opportunity promising high returns with little risk.
- Protect: Conduct thorough research, consult with a financial advisor, and be wary of investments that pressure you to act quickly.

Conclusion

Protecting yourself from scammers and cons requires a combination of vigilance, education, and proactive measures. By understanding the tactics used by scammers, securing your personal information, recognizing red flags, and taking steps to protect your finances and digital footprint, you can significantly reduce your risk of falling victim to scams.

Stay informed, use available resources, and foster a culture of awareness and caution among your family and friends. In the ever-evolving landscape of scams and cons, knowledge and vigilance are your best defenses.

Final Chapter: A Constant Vigilance

In the ever-evolving world of scams and cons, one thing remains constant: there is always a new mark. Scammers are relentless, perpetually refining their tactics and seeking out fresh victims. As technology advances and new vulnerabilities emerge, the landscape of deceit adapts, becoming more sophisticated and harder to detect. This final chapter serves as a stark warning to remain ever-vigilant, stay informed, and protect yourself and your loved ones from the pervasive threat of scams.

The Evolving Threat

1. Continuous Adaptation:

- New Tactics: Scammers continually develop new tactics to exploit unsuspecting individuals. From deepfake technology to AI-generated voices, the tools of deception are becoming increasingly advanced.
- Emerging Technologies: As technology evolves, so do the methods of scamming. Virtual reality, cryptocurrency, and smart devices all present new opportunities for fraudsters.

2. Global Reach:

- Cross-Border Scams: The internet has enabled scammers to operate globally, targeting victims from different countries and jurisdictions. This makes it harder for law enforcement to track and prosecute perpetrators.

- Language and Cultural Barriers: Scammers exploit language and cultural barriers to confuse and deceive victims, making it essential to stay informed about global scam trends.

The Never-Ending Hunt for New Marks

1. The Universal Vulnerability:

- Anyone Can Be a Target: Regardless of age, background, or level of awareness, anyone can fall victim to a scam. Scammers tailor their approaches to exploit the specific vulnerabilities of their targets.
- Human Nature: Trust, empathy, ambition, and desperation are inherent human traits that scammers manipulate to their advantage. These traits make everyone a potential mark.

2. The Cycle of Deception:

- Constant Search: Scammers are always on the lookout for new victims. They use social media, data breaches, and public records to identify and target potential marks.
- Adapting to Awareness: As awareness of certain scams increases, scammers shift their focus and develop new schemes. This cycle ensures that there is always a new mark, unaware of the latest threats.

Staying Ahead of the Scammers

1. Education and Awareness:

- Stay Informed: Regularly educate yourself about new scams and tactics. Follow trusted sources, such as consumer protection agencies, cybersecurity experts, and news outlets.
- Community Sharing: Share information about scams with your community. The more people are aware of potential threats, the harder it becomes for scammers to find new marks.

2. Practical Precautions:

- Secure Your Information: Protect your personal and financial information with strong passwords, two-factor authentication, and regular monitoring.
- Verify Before Trusting: Always verify the legitimacy of requests for money or personal information, especially if they come from unsolicited contacts.

3. Reporting and Cooperation:

- Report Scams: If you encounter a scam, report it to the relevant authorities. Your report can help prevent others from falling victim and assist in the prosecution of scammers.
- Support Victims: Offer support and resources to those who have been scammed. Victims often feel ashamed and isolated, and your support can help them recover.

The Personal Responsibility

1. Vigilance is Key:

- Constant Vigilance: Maintain a healthy level of skepticism, especially when dealing with unfamiliar or unsolicited contacts. Vigilance is your first line of defense against scams.
- Regular Check-Ins: Periodically review your security practices and update them as necessary. Staying ahead of potential threats requires ongoing effort.

2. Empowering Yourself and Others:

- Empowerment Through Knowledge: Empower yourself with knowledge and share it with others. Educate your family, friends, and community about the risks and how to protect themselves.
- Creating a Safe Environment: Foster an environment where people feel comfortable discussing scams and seeking help. Open communication can prevent victimization and promote recovery.

Conclusion

The battle against scams and cons is ongoing, and there will always be a new mark. Scammers are persistent and innovative, exploiting every opportunity to deceive and defraud. However, by staying informed, practicing vigilance, and fostering a culture of awareness and support, we can protect ourselves and our communities from the ever-present threat of scams.

Remember, anyone can be scammed, but with knowledge and caution, we can significantly reduce the risk. Stay vigilant, stay informed, and protect yourself and your loved ones from the relentless pursuit of scammers. In this ever-changing landscape of deceit, our best defense is constant vigilance and a commitment to staying one step ahead.